Grief Diaries

Surviving Loss of a Sibling

True stories about
surviving loss of a sibling

LYNDA CHELDELIN FELL
with
CHRISTINE BASTONE

FOREWORD BY
BENJAMIN SCOTT ALLEN
Out of the Ashes: Healing in the Afterloss

A portion of proceeds from the sale of this book is
donated to The Compassionate Friends, a nonprofit
organization working to provide friendship, understanding and hope to those going through the
natural grieving process. compassionatefriends.org.

Grief Diaries
Surviving Loss of a Sibling – 2nd ed.
An intimate collection of true stories about surviving loss of a sibling.
Lynda Cheldelin Fell/Christine Bastone
Grief Diaries www.GriefDiaries.com

Cover Design by AlyBlue Media, LLC
Interior Design by AlyBlue Media LLC
Published by AlyBlue Media, LLC

ISBN: 978-1-944328-02-3
Library of Congress Control Number: 2015916909
AlyBlue Media, LLC
Ferndale, WA 98248
www.AlyBlueMedia.com

This book is designed to provide informative narrations to readers. It is sold with the understanding that the writers, authors or publisher is not engaged to render any type of psychological, legal, or any other kind of professional advice. The content is the sole expression and opinion of the authors and writers. No warranties or guarantees are expressed or implied by the choice to include any of the content in this book. Neither the publisher nor the author or writers shall be liable for any physical, psychological, emotional, financial, or commercial damages including but not limited to special, incidental, consequential or other damages. Our views and rights are the same: You are responsible for your own choices, actions and results.

PRINTED IN THE UNITED STATES OF AMERICA

GRIEF DIARIES

TESTIMONIALS

"CRITICALLY IMPORTANT . . . I want to say to Lynda that what you are doing is so critically important." –DR. BERNICE A. KING, Daughter of Dr. Martin Luther King

"INSPIRATIONAL . . . Grief Diaries is the result of heartfelt testimonials from a dedicated and loving group of people. By sharing their stories, the reader will find inspiration and a renewed sense of comfort as they move through their own journey." -CANDACE LIGHTNER, Founder of Mothers Against Drunk Driving

"DEEPLY INTIMATE . . . Grief Diaries is a deeply intimate, authentic collection of narratives that speak to the powerful, often ambiguous, and wide spectrum of emotions that arise from loss. I so appreciate the vulnerability and truth embedded in these stories, which honor and bear witness to the many forms of bereavement that arise in the aftermath of death." -DR. ERICA GOLDBLATT HYATT, Chair of Psychology, Bryn Athyn College

"HOPE . . . These stories reflect the authentic voices of individuals at the unexpected moment their lives were shattered and altered forever. Moments of strength in the midst of indescribable pain, resilience in the midst of rage; hope while mired in despair; each of which remind us in law enforcement to uphold our oath to protect and serve by never giving up." —SHERIFF SADIE DARNELL, Alachua County, Florida; Chair, Florida Cold Case Advisory Commission

"BRAVE . . . The brave individuals who share their truth in this book do it for the benefit of all." CAROLYN COSTIN - Founder, Monte Nido Treatment Centers

"ACCURATE . . . These accounts portray an accurate picture of just what full-force repercussions follow the taking of a life." JAY HOWELL, U.S. Senate Investigator, Former Florida State Prosecutor, Co-founder - National Center for Missing & Exploited Children

"VITAL . . . Grief Diaries: Surviving Loss of a Pregnancy gives voice to the thousands of women who face this painful journey every day. Often alone in their time of need, these stories will play a vital role in surrounding each reader with warmth and comfort as they seek understanding and healing in the aftermath of their own loss." -JENNIFER CLARKE, obstetrical R.N., Perinatal Bereavement Committee at AMITA Health Adventist Medical Center

"HOPE AND HEALING . . . You are a pioneer in this field and you are breaking the trail for others to find hope and healing."
-KRISTI SMITH, Bestselling Author & International Speaker

"WONDERFUL . . .Grief Diaries is a wonderful computation of stories written by the best of experts, the bereaved themselves. Thank you for building awareness about a topic so near and dear to my heart."
-DR. HEIDI HORSLEY, Adjunct Professor, School of Social Work, Columbia University, Author, Co-Founder of Open to Hope Organization

"MOVING . . . In Grief Diaries, the stories are not only moving but often provide a rich background for any mourner to find a gem of insight that can be used in coping with loss. Reread each story with pen in hand and you will find many that are just right for you." -DR. LOUIS LAGRAND, Author of Healing Grief, Finding Peace

"HEALING . . . Grief Diaries gives voice to a grief so private, most bear it alone. These diaries can heal hearts and begin to build community and acceptance to speak the unspeakable. Share this book with friends who have faced grief. Pour a cup of tea together and know that you are no longer alone." -DIANNA VAGIANOS ARMENTROUT, Poetry Therapist & Author of Walking the Labyrinth of My Heart: A Journey of Pregnancy, Grief and Infant Death

"STUNNING . . . Grief Diaries treats the reader to a rare combination of candor and fragility through the eyes of the bereaved. Delving into the deepest recesses of the heartbroken, the reader easily identifies with the diverse collection of stories and richly colored threads of profound love that create a stunning read full of comfort and hope." -DR. GLORIA HORSLEY, President, Open to Hope Foundation

DEDICATION

In loving memory of:

Kevin Kyle Boos
Eunice Marie Dettrey
Rob Forestbird
Brian Andrew Habedank
Suzette Yvonne Lee
Donald Levine
Michael Andrew Malone
Austin Jon Park
Timothy Brian Rebe
Elizabeth Noel Sclafani
Patrick Smith
Todd Woinovick

CONTENTS

BY BENJAMIN SCOTT ALLEN

FOREWORD

Our oldest son Matt was almost three when his little brother Bryan died at the age of eight months. Bryan could never crawl or hold his head up on his own and when he died he was basically the size of a newborn. A medical term used for Bryan was he had a "failure to thrive." Bryan would sit in his swing and his eyes would follow Matt wherever he went. Deep blue eyes traced the outer edges and the inner heart of his big brother until his eyes no longer opened. After the funeral, Lydia and I took Matt back to the grave where a mound of dirt rested where once there was a hole the day before. Matt walked straight to the dirt and picked up the largest piece he could wrestle and with a voice of innocence said, "Let's take Bryan home now."

Brothers for eight months. Brothers for a lifetime. Matt lived another ten years and died at the age of thirteen. We had many conversations about a life that entered ours and left an indelible imprint on every breath we took. His love for Bryan never wavered, never subsided in the days and nights living on the precipice of his own life and death. Brothers for life. Brothers for love. Brothers forever.

I was the youngest of three brothers, each entering this earth two years apart. Two years ago, Michael, the oldest, died at the age of sixty-one. A few months ago, Skip died at the age of sixty-one. Brothers for life. Brothers for love. Brothers forever.

I walked with the innocent anguish of a child, my child, in the loss of his brother. I watched as he was losing his life. I watched the rapid decline of my oldest brother and his ultimate death and just a few years beyond that I watched the sudden and not so sudden death of my remaining brother.

There is something about the proximity of the heartbeat of siblings. I observed the physiological, emotional, mental and spiritual intertwining of the layers of the heart as my brothers and I went about our days in the ebb and flow of relationship. Not all of our days were sweetness and light. Not all of our challenges were met in tender loving support. Through the years we drifted apart and returned over and over to the place siblings know – the knowing of each other, the knowing of ourselves, the knowing of that indescribable state of just knowing. We would always return there often, especially in times of both crisis and joy.

In the time I was going through that thirteen-year period of walking with Bryan, Matt and their mother, Lydia, through their deaths, my brother Skip was there. But it was not there where he first arrived. Skip stood over my crib praying I would not die for I, too, was born on the edges of death. Night after night, day after day, Skip held his two-year-old vigil by my bedside just as Matt sat next to Bryan so many years later.

Skip and I were the closest. Michael was always harder to connect with and after he was diagnosed with schizophrenia at the age of nineteen, the pieces fell into place as to why we had such difficulties in our relationship. But all three of us shared the sorrow of Michael's daughter's death just a week before her twenty-fifth birthday. We shared the moving of Michael from one city to where Skip lived for his preparation of death. I needed to return home and even at a distance, we shared Michael's departure from this earth. I knew the call at 3 a.m. was Skip. I knew Michael would die in Skip's arms. I just didn't know that less than two years later Skip would find his way out of his body, too.

My first thought, my very first thought, upon hearing about Skip's death was of all the people he had loved and served through his lifetime, Michael would be the first one waiting. And the first thing Michael would say to Skip was, "Thank you." Skip watched over Michael like he did me the first days of my life and every day since.

Skip and I would often talk of our oldest brother during Michael's life and even more after his death. Skip missed Michael, even with all the extra care Michael needed throughout his life. Skip said to me through his tears, "I miss his five phone calls a day."

Part of my belief system comes from the experience of what happens to me when someone dies. I believe a part of me goes with them and a part of them stays with me. Grief is the reintegration of a new me, a new relationship with the one that has died, and a new relationship with the world I now live in. This world is not of the world I once lived. I am not the person I once was. And our relationship is not over for it continues to evolve and change into a perpetual unfolding of life and love in all its dimensions.

When someone dies, many say they have gone to the afterlife. I was no longer in the life I once lived and I started to describe my new world as the *afterloss*. It is a multilayered experience of life, of joy, of sorrow, of pain, of love, of everything that is now unfolding from what was into what will become.

One part of this landscape of the afterloss is the terrain of shared history. Loss shatters so much, and one of the pieces I needed to lean into was all the experiences we shared and how the voice on the other end of the line knew my heartbeat, my story, my fears, and hopes. Just by the tone of our voices we knew each other's core. We would live from the core and find laughter and tears there.

Skip and I shared everything. Our sharing today has changed. It is in the beginning stages of the evolutionary process, and I have yet to settle into my natural rhythm and pace within the expanse. Through my tears I will always miss the sound of his laughter and the feel of his embrace. I miss his physical presence even as loss takes me beyond the physical.

I am still here. I am the only one left. And I deal with the stretching of my heart across the universe as I am tethered to this place, this place I feel so left behind. Even though they are all here. They are all there. And even though I am still here. I am still there.

Loss contracts me, but ultimately, loss expands me. Skip's loss is so fresh. I know the drill. I know I need stillness and space to lean into my sorrow. I know that the quiet of my afterloss under a blanket of distant stars heals me. I know this time has yet to find its place in the timelessness of my afterloss. And I know it will take time. So I am gentle in this good night. I walk with measured steps and step lightly on to every moving landscape of my afterloss. My sorrow finds respite in the breezes that blow against the tears that flow so freely. In my aloneness, I am not alone.

Of all the people on this planet, I was closest to Skip. We shared a life one moment at a time. We had shared history. We talked every day with laughter and love. Those days are gone and I am in the dusk of our shared history and living the night waiting for dawn.

Every loss hurts. But every loss is different. The ingredients of loss are the same, but my experiences have led me to see that the intensity and focus have their own unique signatures. The loss of my children, the loss of my first wife, the loss of my mother, and the loss of my brothers all feel different, but the same. The same texture unfolds within a unique touch.

The world of my afterloss has taught me so much, given me so much, and taken so much. One of the greatest gifts I have experienced is the reality that love never dies. I am so grateful that what loss leaves me is love itself and the ever-unfolding of love in its expanse.

Life can hurt. Loss can hurt. Love can hurt. But when I choose to lean into life, loss, and love I walk within a mystical union with their very essence. I am transformed in the transformational experiences of the life we had and have, the losses we have gone and are going through, and the love that keeps unfolding.

Brothers for life. Brothers for love. Brothers forever.

BENJAMIN SCOTT ALLEN
Author, *Out of the Ashes: Healing in the Afterloss*
www.TheAfterLoss.com

BY LYNDA CHELDELIN FELL

PREFACE

One night in 2007, I had a vivid dream. I was the front passenger in a car and my teen daughter Aly was sitting behind the driver. Suddenly, the car missed a curve in the road and sailed into a lake. The driver and I escaped the sinking car, but Aly did not. As I bobbed to the surface, I dove again and again in the murky water desperately searching for my daughter. But I failed to find her. She was gone. My beloved daughter was gone, leaving nothing but an open book floating on the water where she disappeared.

Two years later, on August 5, 2009, that horrible nightmare became reality when Aly died as a backseat passenger in a car accident. Returning home from a swim meet, the car carrying Aly was T-boned by a father coming home from work. My beautiful fifteen-year-old daughter took the brunt of the impact and died instantly. She was the only fatality.

Just when I thought life couldn't get any worse, it did. My dear sweet hubby buried his grief in the sand. He escaped into eighty-hour workweeks, more wine, more food, and less talking. His blood pressure shot up, his cholesterol went off the chart, and the perfect storm arrived on June 4, 2012, when he suddenly began drooling and couldn't speak. My 46-year-old soulmate was having a major stroke.

My husband survived the stroke but couldn't speak, read, or write, and his right side was paralyzed. Still reeling from the loss of our daughter, I found myself again thrust into a fog of grief so thick I couldn't see through the storm. Adrenaline and autopilot resumed their familiar place at the helm.

In the aftermath, I eventually discovered that helping others was a powerful way to heal my own heart. The Grief Diaries series was born and built on this belief. By writing books narrating our journeys, our written words become a portable support group for others who share our path. When we swap stories, we feel less alone. It is comforting to know someone else understands the shoes we walk in, and the challenges we face along the way.

Which brings us to this book, *Grief Diaries: Surviving Loss of a Sibling*. Helen Keller once said, "Walking with a friend in the dark is better than walking alone in the light." This is especially true in the aftermath of sibling loss, because it's often cast into the shadows while the focus sits squarely on the bereaved parents. Make no mistake—sibling loss is a devastating, life-changing experience. To lose a sibling is to lose part of yourself and your childhood.

For anyone who has lost a sibling, the following stories are written by people who know exactly how you feel because they've worn your shoes. Although no two journeys are identical, we hope you'll find comfort in our stories and the understanding that you aren't truly alone, for we walk ahead, behind, and right beside you.

Wishing you healing and hope from the Grief Diaries village.

Warm regards,

Lynda Cheldelin Fell

Creator, Grief Diaries
www.LyndaFell.com

CHAPTER ONE

THE BEGINNING

Infinity is a way to describe the incomprehensible to
the human mind. In a way, it notates a mystery. That
kind of mystery exists in relationships. A lifetime is not
enough to know someone else. It provides a brief
glimpse. -SIMON MCBURNEY

Grief and sorrow is unique to each individual as his or her fingerprint. In order to fully appreciate one's perspective, it is helpful to
understand one's journey. In this chapter each writer shares that
moment when each lost his or her sibling to help you understand
when life as they knew it ended, and a new one began.

*

EMILY BAIRD-LEVINE
Emily's 43-year-old brother Don
died from a heart attack in 2004

My brother Don, of blessed memory, was a very lovable,
funny, giving, intelligent person. He easily adapted to any new
social or learning situation with enthusiasm. He had the ability to
make people comfortable. Don was truly a *mensch,* which is Yiddish
for someone of consequence; someone to admire and emulate; an
upright, honorable, decent person. Or, as a rabbi of ours once said,
"A mensch is someone who does the right thing, at the right time,

for the right reason." This sums up Don very well. He was a good friend to many who adored him, a wonderful brother, a dedicated and loving son, and a fun uncle to his nieces and nephews. Don often gave gifts of rubber chickens and glow stick glasses!

Don was the valedictorian of his high school graduating class. He earned his B.A. in Economics from Pomona College and worked as an acquisitions analyst for a company that managed investments for low income housing projects.

Don was diagnosed with type I diabetes at age three. This was at a time when glucometers to test blood sugar did not exist. Blood sugar was tested with urine tests that indicated what one's blood sugar was twenty-four hours prior. This was also a time when diabetics were not allowed to eat sugar or participate in rigorous exercise. Don played like every other kid, but I recall that when he got to middle school he wasn't allowed to do much in P.E. class and he was the batboy for the baseball team. The coach and players all loved Don and he enjoyed helping out.

It was about this time when I started noticing that my brother, who was two-and-a-half years older, was shorter than I was. I never quite understood why. I know that for years Don went to our pediatrician, Dr. Diamond, to manage the diabetes. Somewhere down the road, Dr. Diamond retired and it seemed that neither one of us went back to a doctor for a long time. I believe Don was around seventeen or eighteen when he started to complain about his eyesight. My mom took both of us to the eye doctor and my exam went well but Don's did not. We were informed at that eye appointment that Don had diabetic retinopathy, along with other complications from the diabetes. He was immediately admitted to the hospital. His kidneys were failing, he was put on dialysis, and his insulin intake needed to be managed.

Don was in and out the hospital for an extended amount of time during his senior year of high school. He went for dialysis several times a week. He did start college and had to drop out for a year to have a kidney transplant. My oldest brother, Andy, donated a kidney to Don. This kidney gave Don an extra twenty-four years of life that he wouldn't otherwise have had. Don was put on prednisone after that transplant. This is necessary because it is used as an anti-rejection medication. Unfortunately, steroids are very difficult on internal organs and on blood sugar.

Don was able to fine tune management of his blood sugar while taking prednisone but over time the effects of the steroids took a toll on his lungs specifically. He would get sick often, and a few days before he passed away he was doing breathing treatments but they weren't helping. Don ultimately lost too much oxygen and had a heart attack. Between the damage to his brain and the heart attack, he didn't make it.

*

CHRISTINE BASTONE
Christine's 38-year-old sister
Liz died by suicide in 2012

My baby sister, Elizabeth Noel Shively, was born on December 5, 1973, to my parents Kay and Jim Shively. She has two older sisters: me, of course, Christine, otherwise known as Cricket, and Pamela, otherwise known as Pam. Elizabeth was named after our grandmother who died a week before Liz was born. She was actually born a few weeks early and was so small that you could lay her across one of our dining room chairs without her hanging over the edges. Liz grew up to be five foot two, with eyes of blue. And sadly she always thought that she was too short. I really wish that she would have somehow realized that she wasn't too short, but that she was just right.

3

When Liz was a toddler she climbed into a bathtub of water with all of her clothes on, including shoes. My mother had to take a picture, and it's absolutely priceless. Liz is looking up with a look of pure innocence on her face. It's my favorite picture of her, and I have it as the background on my desktop computer. It's classic Liz...a little bit different, with a look that says, "Why are you looking at me like that?"

Every summer for a good part of my childhood my family and I would vacation at a two-bedroom condo in Fort Myers, Florida, for about a month. As my parents shared the master bedroom and Pam and I shared the second one, Liz ended up sleeping in a big walk-in closet. It's better than it sounds as she got to have a space all her own, and it was absolutely perfect for the size that Liz was at the time.

While I always thought it was pretty, Liz never liked her middle name. "Noel" means Christmas in French, and she thought it was kind of stupid to have a name that means a holiday. Sometime during her early years, my father tried to nickname her "George." Liz was called that for a little while but it didn't really stick. Instead she became known as "Liz."

There were many Sundays when my sisters and I would visit our great-aunt Irene and great-uncle Jack's house. There were lots of fun things to play with there, especially in their basement. But the absolute best part about going there was having ice cream and watermelon. They had this really nice sunroom, and we would eat sitting at a round coffee table in the center of it. Liz loved the ice cream and watermelon the most of us three kids.

Liz was bold, beautiful, and outspoken. And, oh boy, was she funny! I can't tell you how many times I have chuckled while reading over a copy of some of the surveys that she posted on

MySpace. I now wish that I had saved every one of them that she did. Liz was also full of life. I look at pictures of her now, and that just shines through. But she was also difficult. Normally it takes two people to fight, but not with her. She would follow you around the house talking about whatever it was that she was upset about until you couldn't take it anymore, and you yelled at her. How I miss that! I'd give a lot to have Liz here being difficult once again.

I think the trait that was her undoing was her negative thinking. Liz was probably the most negative thinker I ever knew, and that includes myself! Another trait that certainly didn't help her was her perfectionism. I mean all five of us in the Shively family are perfectionists to one degree or another. But what I didn't realize until sometime after Liz died was that she may very well have been the biggest perfectionist of us all.

On June 29, 2001, Liz married a guy named Adam Sclafani. And in December 2002, Liz had her only child, a son she adored named Damian. When Damian was very young, Liz and Adam moved to Canada for Adam's job. She was there for about a year, and was very unhappy there. She was really isolated with a young child. She was away from almost everything and everyone whom she loved. And the bad weather in the winter only helped to increase her sense of isolation. Liz then moved to Michigan and then a few years later back to Ohio. Moving that many times was certainly very stressful for her, although she definitely did a much better job than I could have ever done at organizing said moves!

My sister had quite an awesome singing voice. Around 2008 or so she started participating in MySpace Karaoke. I had absolutely no idea that she could sing like that, and I really enjoyed listening to her. It is such a shame that MySpace Karaoke doesn't exist anymore, and all that lovely music is gone now.

one who passed was the best person there was, and in my case I say it with confidence. Kevin was so loving, so understanding, and so patient. He wasn't perfect, but he was as close as it gets. There were many people who wouldn't be given a second glance by most, but he never gave up on them. A lot of people gave up on me, but Kevin never left my side. I am forever grateful to him.

Kevin spent two years studying at Florida State University in Tallahassee (pursuing a music degree, of course). He loved the school, the Seminoles, the city, the atmosphere. If it was related to FSU, he was all about it. He spent one year as president of Epsilon Sigma Alpha, which is a co-ed service fraternity. He was constantly attending and running community service events, raising money, supporting the homeless, and doing all kinds of incredible things that the average person would never do.

When we were younger, I was Kevin's "protector." Though I was sixteen months younger, I took the older sister role. He was very shy, sensitive, and quiet. My parents even had Kevin tested for autism, but doctors weren't able to diagnose him with it.

I was always so worried about him, even while we were in college together. However, as soon as he left high school he grew into his own and became a confident, strong man who I hadn't known before. His successes were incredible in the short time he was at FSU, and he worked so incredibly hard towards his dreams. Unfortunately, Kevin didn't get into the music program at FSU for reasons we'll never know. We all knew how heartbroken he was, but again he made something great out of it. He moved home to southern Florida and moved in with our brother, Jeffrey. This is when he began working as a busboy, and really started focusing on his music. While most people would have given up on their passion after that kind of rejection, Kevin used it to fuel himself to work even harder. Every single day he worked on his music, made money on the side, and had that big grin on his face no matter what life threw at him.

On the weekend of September 6, 2015, Kevin and a few friends traveled up to Florida State to spend Labor Day weekend with friends. He was so excited to see everyone again, to attend a football game, and to have fun in his favorite city. That Sunday night, Kevin and his three friends, Morgan, Vincenzo, and Niko, left the friend's apartment to go get food. What they didn't know was that someone they never met made the selfish, disgusting decision to get behind the wheel of a car after drinking too much.

I was at my new apartment in Gainesville with friends. I had just been on the phone with my mom and we hung up. She called back not even five minutes later, and I will never forget her words.

"Shannon. There was an accident."

"What? Where?"

"In Tallahassee. Kevin was in the car, I don't know who else. I'm on the way to the hospital, apparently it's not good."

My roommates drove me the two hours to Tallahassee. During the drive I kept frantically calling my mom, my dad, my brother, hoping for answers. I texted Kevin, telling him I would be there soon. I had plans to buy him his favorite candy and a stupid little teddy bear, thinking he would be hospitalized for a while.

He never made it to the hospital.

After the longest ride of my life, I jumped out of the car before it even came to a stop. I threw open the emergency room door, screaming at the first person I saw, "My brother was in an accident! Where is he?"

"Who's your brother?"

"Kevin Boos."

I should've known then by the look on the police officer's face. His look was filled with nothing but guilt and heartbreak. I refused to believe it.

I thought to myself, okay, he's probably unconscious and injured. I need to prepare myself to see him hooked up to machines.

Instead, I was taken to one of those family counseling rooms, the kind nobody wants to go into. You know the ones — you see it in the movies when someone dies. But my brother wasn't dead. Why is he bringing me in here?

I was greeted by some random woman, and my mother. She looked lifeless. My mother, who was always so happy to see me with sunshine pouring out of her eyes, wasn't there.

She sat me down and shut the door. I still didn't want to believe what was coming.

"He's gone."

Screaming.

Nothing but screaming.

Were they my screams? My mom's?

My face was soaking wet. My tears combined with those from my mother — a mother who had just lost her child.

It wasn't just my brother and friends who died that day. My life ended too.

At 9:15 p.m. on Sunday, September 6, 2015, Kevin and his two friends, Vincenzo and Morgan, were all killed by a drunk driver. And that is when our world stopped.

*

LISA FORESTBIRD
Lisa's 40-year-old brother Rob died
from a pontine hemorrhage in 2006

Rob was my magical older brother. He indeed did play magician at my eighth birthday party, but what made him magic is that he had a special way of making me feel everything was okay. Also, he was extremely fun to be around. When I had an important decision to make or I was struggling in school, my parents sent me to Rob. I have no idea why my family and I relied so much on Rob, but we did. He was brilliant and I suppose in some ways we thought he was more capable than we were to handle issues ranging from Apple computing to making travel arrangements.

When we were little, Rob liked to be boss. Some may call it bullying, but I just call it growing up with two brothers. If Rob decided we needed a dunk while swimming, we would get a dunk. He'd make fun of me when formal occasions would require me to wear a dress or a skirt, and he used to make "boo boxes" using cardboard soda boxes, tissue paper and paper towel tubes. When we were really little it seemed appropriate to boo at our siblings' special occasions because, after all, if it wasn't our occasion we weren't getting attention, gifts, and special treatment.

As we got older Rob developed different hobbies and interests. When I was in junior high, we formed a secret "Teacher Information Club" which surely was one hundred percent his idea. He would assign me surveillance tasks and I would win points and accolades for performing various challenges such as getting kicked out of the classroom or placing my feet on my reading teacher's designer furniture. I suppose he did it because he was bored. I did it because I adored my older brother and would pretty much do anything he told me to do.

I'm pretty sure Rob's oldest child persona transferred into his professional life. He was a hard-driving and life-loving anesthesiologist which was likely the death of him. He drank too much Mountain Dew and abandoned his blood pressure medicine for reasons completely unknown to us. He loved to travel and aside from being an accomplished professional, people loved him because he was nice and caring and had great people skills. Although Rob had his quirky hobbies, described above, as a youngster, he was quite the serious fellow. I was the class clown and my parents said with the passage of time, Rob soaked up some of my *joie de vivre* and I learned the art of occasionally taking life seriously from him.

Two weekends before Rob went into a coma, we had spent a glorious Labor Day weekend together. Rob came to Michigan to pick up my Miata and drive it to Washington for me. He planned to take the northern route west, because the weather permitted it and it was a route he had never taken. His girlfriend, Molly, was extremely worried about Rob making the trip, but we all brushed her concerns aside. I remember sitting in the passenger's seat of the Miata with Rob in the driver's seat, me watching him Windex the windows before he left. I remember wondering what would become of Molly and Rob. Would they get married? Would they just keep dating forever? I also remember telling Rob I was going to be okay. I was finally getting my act together and was positive about my future course. I remember the night before, coming home in tears over a romantic situation, and Rob just looking into my eyes...both concerned and probably befuddled. But I remember the intensity of his stare. Rob and Molly left that gorgeous Michigan sunny afternoon, and in the days ahead, Rob gave me frequent status reports on my Miata. I gave him strict instructions to not lower the convertible roof, because it was ripping.

The day before we got the call, Rob called me to say he had changed the oil in his car. Only later did I realize Rob took better care of my car...his patients...his family than he did himself. We will never know why.

On Tuesday, September 12, 2006, I was at my legal aid hotline job on the phone with a gentlemen when my cellphone rang. My dad never called me at work and it was rare I would even pay attention to my cellphone while on the clock but for some reason I took the call. He said Rob had passed out at Yellowstone. I asked him why he was calling me as it was probably just Rob playing a joke. He told me to come home and when my boss asked me if I would be okay, I insisted I would be fine as my brother had both a doctor and a nurse at his side. When I got home my parents were talking about making immediate arrangements to fly to Idaho Falls to be with Rob. We called the hospital and a very nice chaplain let me talk to Rob and he assured me Rob could hear everything I was saying. On the way to the airport we got a call from one of Rob's partners. He said Rob wasn't going to make it. Somehow, I already knew that. Rob was in a coma for six days before passing away.

The only thing that made sense to me was that Rob was a gift. He was only meant to be on this earth for forty years and that explained why he lived life so intensely.

*

BONNIE FORSHEY
Bonnie's 54-year-old sister Eunice
died from bladder cancer in 2010

My sister and I were discarded when we were very young. We were abused by our stepfather as toddlers and suffered immensely at his hands. We should have been loved, encouraged and praised. Instead we were beat, tortured, and locked in a closet. I remember so many incidents and how I tried to console my sister, but I was just a child myself. One day Eunice was hit by a car trying to retrieve a toy that our stepfather had thrown into the street. One day she was wearing a beautiful angora hat, and he set it on fire while it was on her head. My mother burned her hands pulling it off. I remember so much. My sister was my joy and I loved her.

On the last day of kindergarten we were taken to Delaware to begin a new life with people who we had never seen before. We were told that they were our grandmother and father. We were finally safe and we flourished. There was plenty to eat, no more crying or beatings, and no more closets. I protected my sister and read to her, and held her when she was sad. But we both missed our mother and couldn't understand what we had done to make her give us away. Throughout the years, I walked to school with Eunice and took her to class. I protected her against bullies, helped her with homework, and became her "mother." We remained close throughout our adult lives and spoke almost every day. When I lost my sixteen-year-old son Billy in 1993, Eunice was there for me, and she encouraged me to go on. I became an R.N., and Eunice became an L.P.N. She started telling me about certain symptoms she was having and I begged her to see a doctor. She wouldn't listen and thought she could handle things on her own. She was embarrassed because one of the problems was incontinence, and she didn't want anyone to know. Oh, how I wish that she would've listened to me.

Eunice began having mini strokes and later they found a tumor in her sinus cavity. Other problems intensified until she could not urinate. We took her to the hospital and they took her in for exploratory surgery. The doctor came out and told me they found a mass in her bladder, it was cancer. He said he could remove it, including her bladder, and that Eunice would have to have a urostomy. He said that he would schedule the surgery.

We took Eunice home and I advised her to seek a second opinion. She went to an oncologist and he sent her for a PET scan. When he came out to speak to me, I knew by the expression on his face that it was not good news. The cancer was not contained and it had metastasized and was invading her body. I know that I was in shock. All I could think about was my "baby," my sister, her children and my life without her. I wanted it to be a bad dream. I could not bear to see the look on her face when we had to tell her.

How could I go on without her? Oh, how I hated life. Where was God throughout our lives? How could he allow this to happen? Hadn't we been through enough? She was the bravest person that I have ever known. She was so scared but managed to smile, laugh, and joke her way through the chemo and illness. Eunice was so sick and unable to eat. She lost half of her body weight and began to put her affairs in order. I took her to her appointments, set up hospice, and did everything possible to keep her comfortable.

Eunice could not breathe without oxygen now. She started having a problem urinating and I took her back to the hospital and they admitted her. I tried to keep Eunice's spirits up, but we both knew that she was fighting a losing battle. They brought her a food tray and she kept looking at it with a puzzled look on her face. It dawned on me that she was "lost" and didn't know what to do. I cut up her food and put the fork in her hand. She still didn't know what to do, so I began to feed her. She looked up at me and began to cry. She said, "I'm not going to walk out of here. Take care of my boys." I began to cry and held her close to me. Oh God, why her? Take me instead, I begged, under my breath.

The next day, they moved Eunice to ICU as she had started having mini strokes again. She was on life support. I held her hand, stroked her forehead, and kissed her cheek. All of a sudden all of the alarms were going off and just like that, my sister was gone. Apparently a blood clot had hit her heart. I lost a huge part of myself and life will never be the same.

*

LAURA HABEDANK
Laura's brother Brian died
by suicide in 2010 at age 35

My life was irreversibly changed on October 13, 2010, when I received the call from my mom confirming that my brother had been found dead in his home. He had taken his own life.

I learned of his lifelong struggle with depression only five months earlier when he confided in me that he had attempted suicide twice before. I spent the following months regularly reaching out to him, arranging for therapy appointments and panicking each time a phone call or text went unanswered, fearing the worst. I felt so helpless being so far away. He was living in my home state of Minnesota, and I had relocated to Texas less than a year earlier. I was desperately trying to save his life, and even went so far as to ask Brian to promise me that he wouldn't hurt himself. He told me that was a promise he could not keep.

Throughout the day on October 13, Brian was not responding to any emails, text messages or phone calls. After a number of family members pieced details together, we determined that no one had been in contact with Brian since a week earlier. We made the decision to send the police to his home for a wellness check, and they confirmed our worst fears. The medical examiner said he had likely been dead nearly a week before he was found. My life was completely turned upside down, and I've spent the last five years learning to live in this "new normal." One of the ways I cope is by writing letters to Brian; it helps me process my feelings and feel as though I'm still able to connect with him in a way. Here is the first letter I wrote him a few months after his death:

Dear Brian,

I'll never forget the last time I saw you. It was July 5, 2010. You brought me back to the airport after my visit home for Mom's birthday. The entire ride was so heartbreaking; I could feel it– your profound sadness. I tried to get you to talk about it but you kept changing the subject... so I let it be. I just wanted to spend time with you. I didn't want the ride to end; the closer we got to the airport the more anxious I grew. I didn't want to say goodbye to you– something was happening that made my heart ache for you but I couldn't put my finger on it exactly. You got out to help me with my bags, I gave you a hug and said, "Come visit me soon, okay?? See ya later, dude." Once inside the airport doors I allowed myself to turn around in time to see you driving away; I started sobbing because in my heart I knew I'd never see you again. And I didn't.

That part still haunts me– that I was so connected with you that I could sense that but yet I didn't feel it the moment you died. It will take me a lifetime to get past that an entire week passed before you were found. I felt like I let you down; not only did you die alone but you continued to lie there alone for a week while I went about my life. "He's gone, honey." Those are the first words I heard from Mom confirming that what we had hoped hadn't happened, really had. The nightmare began. For weeks I would call your cellphone several times a day just to hear your voicemail message; I worry that I'll forget the sound of your voice. I was a mess the first time I called your number after it was finally disconnected; it was like you had died all over again and the last remaining connection I had to hearing your voice again was gone.

I keep running through our life together over and over in my head. We were so close in age that we shared everything together; we experienced all stages of life at the same time: childhood . . . high school . . . college . . . jobs . . .everything. And we even liked each other enough to choose to be roommates as adults! I loved that we were not just brother and sister, but we were friends. We included each other in our circles of friends and activities. I keep trying to remember those things: our Sundays watching the Simpsons, you "singing" me the X-Files theme song, pizza and football games, and even you trying, very patiently, to teach me how to drive a manual transmission! You had the most amazing, contagious laugh and a very gentle spirit and are going to be missed by so many people—more than you could have ever imagined. It may not make sense but it feels like you have taken that past with you... and it also feels as though you have also taken my future as I never imagined it without you.

I often wonder how long it'll be before those memories bring me more joy than pain because right now it hurts to think of them. My heart is broken! I find myself detaching from the world, I'm suffering from frequent panic attacks when the pain is just so strong it takes my breath away. I have become jealous of others who have siblings who are still here—and I'm hurt when I see them angry with each other. I am not the same person anymore; I feel so isolated, so different from everyone else. I can laugh . . . but have no true joy right now. I suppose some happiness will come back someday . . . but for now there's only a hole in my heart where you used to be.

Please know that I am not angry at you now nor do I think I ever will be. I have been to that place myself before and fought my way back out. I know it wasn't a compulsive choice you made but rather the culmination of years and years of battling a crippling depression and you held on as long as you could—for us.

I miss you and think of you every waking moment. Instead of saying goodbye to you, since I know I'll see you again, I'll just say what we always said to each other: "See ya later, dude."

Your loving sister,
Laura

*

MARCELLA MALONE
Marcella's 20-year-old brother
Michael died by suicide in 2014

Just fifteen months younger than me, it was inevitable that Michael and I would grow up really close to each other. Up until middle school we were best friends. Many of our friends were even the same. I was into his favorite activities, like participating in a variety of sports, hunting, fishing, and select video games (they were never my strong suit). He traded off and did crafts and played house with me. We had outside friends, but at the end of the day all we needed was each other.

When Michael was in middle school and I in high school, we began to spend less time around each other, but remained close. Until the end, we took on caregiving roles with each other. I spoiled him by cooking for him, driving him around, helping him with chores, picking up his tab most times, packing for him. In turn, he protected me, making sure I was always happy and safe. We told each other most things.

Following high school and the events that led up to Michael not being able to follow his dream of playing college football, he went through a brief down period, but he had seemed to be doing much better the past year or so. He was back to his goofy, fun-loving, super caring self who strove to live life to its fullest.

Michael was working with our dad in Operating Engineers Union Local 324 and making great money. In late March we had a week-long family vacation in Florida. We had a great time and I was thankful for the time I was able to spend with him, as life made these occurrences much less frequent than I had liked. Everything seemed to be going well for Michael — he seemed happy.

19

Fast-forward a couple of weeks to Monday, April 14, 2014. It started out as a normal day. I texted Michael in the morning to make plans to go with him to pick out my baby shower present and talk about the rebuilding of the local FFA barn. Michael was helping my dad paint the upstairs of the house.

When I got out of class, I checked my Facebook page and noticed an unusual post from Michael: "To all those who love me, thank you for showing me what love is." I immediately knew something was wrong. I called and texted Michael repeatedly with no reply. I then began trying to get hold of his friends and our family to see if anyone knew anything. Everyone was just as worried, and many were out searching for Michael. I was two hours away and had class in the morning. I felt completely helpless. I tried to talk to those close to me about my fears, as it was unlike Michael to behave like that, but everyone seemed to feel I was overthinking it. I tried to stay positive and to remember a couple of years earlier when Michael was down and would just go hide out at the lake or a friend's house to take a break. I hoped that would be true again.

I took a bath to relax. When I got out I didn't have time to dry off before I heard the phone ring. It was our dad. Hoping for good news, I quickly answered the phone. The pain in his voice was unbearable as he said, "Michael's dead. He shot himself."

The police found his body and had just come to notify my parents. I immediately dropped my phone and towel; I couldn't believe what I had heard. I was speechless and couldn't even produce a tear. My roommate heard the phone fall and came to check on me. She helped me pack what I needed, as my brain was too scattered for even such a simple task.

During the last snowfall of the year I drove to my parents' house. Through the tears, I sat with them, my older brother and my sister-in-law in complete silence as we tried to prepare for what proved to be the hardest week of our lives. None of our lives would ever be the same.

My brain was overwhelmed with questions of why and what if for a long time. It's hard to explain how it has changed my life. It's almost a year and a half later, and I still struggle daily. My anxiety is definitely much greater, as well as my struggle to trust others; I feel like they will never understand. However, it has also given me a passion toward a future career path, and made me much more perceptive to the emotions of others.

No matter the pain I feel, each day I make it a point to try to make others smile, because you never know what others are going through. Through all the bad I found good, because I know Michael wouldn't want to see me in pain.

The hardest thing is remembering that I will never see him. His nephew, whom Michael was so excited about, will never get the chance to meet him. But life must go on, and for Michael, my guardian angel, I have to do my best to "live big."

*

BROOKE NINNI MATTHEWS
Brooke's 31-year-old brother Timothy
died by homicide in 2012

My brother Timothy was eight years younger than I. He was so loving and loved his family. He tried to protect his sisters, when all his sisters wanted to do was to protect him, and for him to protect himself. Timothy loved to play poker with his buddies. He was a tree trimmer and loved trees and nature. He loved going on vacation to the beach with our family and at times took friends with us. He was quite a jokester, too. I lost my only brother on February

10, 2012, from multiple gunshot wounds to the back, just six months after our mother lost her battle to diabetes and heart disease.

Every Thursday night Timothy would get together with buddies and play poker. Each week they took turns as to where poker was going to be played. On the night of February 9, my brother was playing poker with some of his buddies. It was getting late, like wee hours of the morning. My brother decided to leave the poker game and go to a local bar to meet up with a girl he had been dating for about three days. They left the local bar and decided to go back to her place, and she then invited some people to come back to her place along with them. When they arrived at her place, she and Timothy got into a disagreement and Timothy left. He then called her cellphone to see if he could come back and talk things through. One of the guys she invited back to her place picked up her cellphone and told Timothy that he could come back. When he got back to her place, she had no intentions on talking to my brother. One of the two guys she invited back went outside with my brother and a fight broke out. The fight lasted for some time, until the other guy came outside the girl's house with a gun. He shot my brother seven times, back to front. My brother died there on the cold, wet ground while most of the people took off! One person there fought with another girl to come back, so she could use her phone to call 911! Only one person out of several wanted to stay there and help my brother; she was the last to see Timothy alive. He died scared, alone, no loving family or people around him! His death still haunts me almost four years later.

The perpetrator was sentenced to fifteen to forty years in a state prison, but there will never be closure or peace. It is something I will never understand or get over.

*

NICKI NOBLE
Nicki's 43-year-old brother Don
died from a heart attack in 2004

My funny, kind, intelligent brother Don will always be in my heart. He made me laugh. He was an adorable little boy, which allowed him to be naughty at times and not really ever get in trouble with our parents. He loved puns, Halloween costumes, comedy, *Mad Magazine*, and Jeopardy. Don had many health problems, but he never let that stop him from living life to the fullest. He traveled, explored, and gathered friends and family often. He had funny sayings, costumes such as glow in the dark glasses, rubber chickens, rubber duckies, wigs, and funny hats. I loved to call Don on the phone and listen to his adventures, stories, and jokes. I miss him so much. I want so badly to call him and listen to him just one more time.

As far as his career, Don was very smart and great with numbers. He worked for a company analyzing real estate deals for low income housing projects. He was a very giving and thoughtful person especially for those less fortunate. I believed he liked his job, but he liked to play more.

As far as the circumstances leading up to his death, that is a lifelong story for him. Don was diagnosed with type I diabetes at age three. By age eighteen, he had complete renal failure. My older brother donated a kidney to Don in 1980. The poor diabetic control combined with the steroids needed to keep Don's body from rejecting the new kidney led to pulmonary issues. His heart was very severely affected, and he suffered a heart attack.

He did have a beautiful and kind woman in his life until the very end. I believe they were soul mates. I am so sad they never got the chance to grow old together. They were very much in love and it made me so happy to see him happy.

*

BRIDGET PARK
Bridget's brother Austin died
by suicide in 2008 at age 14

My brother was never the stereotypical suicidal person who wore black or slit his wrists, but rather was very good at being just the opposite. He was his freshman class president and a football player whom all the girls drooled over. I was his dorky younger sister who wore matching sweat outfits, had greasy hair, and embarrassed her older brother at any given moment.

It was a cold November day on the ranch, and just like every Saturday, my brother and I were assigned chores by my parents. I could tell that Austin was high-strung that day or a little less patient, but it was nothing I thought too much about. After a long day of work, we were covered in cow manure and dirt. Since it was Saturday, there was a chance to go to church that evening and to attend the 4:30 p.m. mass that was offered in our small hometown. Being the devout Catholic family that we were, we never missed church. So when we finished chores, we all rushed inside to clean up. However, I guess we didn't hurry fast enough, because when it was time for us to leave, Austin was still in the shower and I had yet to go. My parents, for the first time, let my brother and me miss church. But of course they left us with a list of chores they wanted to be completed by their return. After my shower, Austin and I set out to start our first chore of the evening, which was to clean the kitchen. There was not much to do other than a few dishes and to wipe the counters. I was not really in a hurry, but Austin sure was. I had never seen him clean so fast before with such determination.

Girls and friends kept texting and calling him, asking if he wanted to go out that evening. He just ignored the buzzes of his phone and continued to wipe the counter furiously. At this point I just assumed he was having an off day. As we finished the chore Austin kept saying, "I want to watch TV in Mom and Dad's room," repeatedly. I thought nothing of this other than that he wanted the big TV and the big comfy bed. I followed him to the door of my parents' bedroom and said, "Let me know if you need anything, Austin." I failed to hear the lock of the door click behind him. About fifteen minutes later, I received a call from our cousin asking to speak with Austin. I left my room, passed our living room, turned down the TV I had blasted with my favorite show, and started toward my parent's bedroom. I reached for the doorknob and started to turn it, but it was locked. I casually thought that Austin was just on the phone with a girl or was dancing to his latest favorite tune. I opened a door that led outside and was across from a second door into the bedroom. I immediately saw something red through the glass door. I approached the second bedroom door and there I saw my older brother on his back and a rifle next to him. I had never seen someone look so pale, so translucent. I fell to the ground in fear, thinking someone was there at my home, because my brother would never harm himself in any manner, so it had to be someone else's doing. I never imagined that something so terrible, so tragic, would ever happen to my picture-perfect family.

For years it was a foggy memory until I allowed it to be translucent. Once I did so, I was able to begin healing and growing. I was able to not be ashamed of my brother and my past, because I learned that by helping and sharing my story with others, it just happens to be the way I grieve best and most healthily.

*

MARYELLEN ROACH
MaryEllen's 41-year-old sister Suzette
died in a car accident in 2012

My sister Suzette was born May 13, 1971, and was my parent's only child at the time. I came along seven years later and Suzette was beyond excited to get a little sister to help take care of. She even called me her baby. Although we were seven years apart, we were always pretty close and played together and talked. As we grew up, Suzette never really minded me tagging along with her and, in fact, I think she enjoyed having me with her. I remember one particular time when she was in high school. It was after school and we were standing with some of her friends in the hallway by the gymnasium. Suzette's friends were saying how cute they thought I was and she looked so proud and agreed with them. After Suzette graduated high school and went off to college, she would let me spend some weekends with her and her friends at their campus apartment. We would play games, talk, laugh, go shopping, eat Chinese food (Suzette's favorite), and just have a great time together. I never felt like I didn't belong.

In looking back, college was one of the happiest times in Suzette's life and I'm blessed to have those memories. She graduated from college with a B.A. in Psychology in 1993, and began working. She lived in her own apartment that was located halfway between her job and my parents' home.

Suzette married in September 1998. She and her husband bought their first home in St. Louis, Missouri, shortly after. Suzette desperately wanted a baby and after several miscarriages, she gave birth to Lillian Rose on November 7, 2003. Her second daughter, Vivian Yvonne, was born May 20, 2006. Their family was complete until Suzette noticed abuse and moved with Lillian and Vivian to my parents' home in Illinois. She and her husband divorced in 2008. My parents were thrilled to have her and the girls there so they could spend more time together. Suzette, the girls and I would go to concerts, the park, the zoo, and other places together. Our family had combined birthday parties in March, May, and October. We were all a close knit family.

Suzette still worked the night shift in St. Louis which was about seventy miles from my parents' home. Luckily, my house was only a mile from the children's psychiatric hospital where Suzette worked, so she stayed with me during the week instead of driving home tired. She had her own room at my house and since I was working while she needed to sleep, the house was quiet and it worked perfectly. Everyone was content with the living arrangements and we thought that's how life would be for a while.

Unfortunately, everything changed on July 26, 2012. It started when I got a call from my mom that night around 11 p.m. She was wondering if Suzette and the girls had stopped by my house after their early evening appointment in St. Louis. Suzette wasn't answering her phone which was unusual and they should have been home hours earlier. Suzette was always good about letting everyone know if she would be later than expected, but neither of us had heard from her. Mom said she was going to call Suzette again and let me know when she got in touch with her. When mom called back forty-five minutes later, I thought she was calling to tell me they had arrived home, but when I heard the tone in her voice...I knew. Although I wish I could forget the words she said, I don't think I ever will. "MaryEllen. The sheriff is here and Suzette and the girls were in an accident." My mind raced with the thought of, "Okay, what hospital are they in? If they're in St. Louis, I'm close. If they're in Illinois, I need to pack clothes and I'll be on my way." But my mom's next words were, "and they're all dead." As soon as I heard those words, I felt a separation happen. It felt like I was looking down at myself, seeing myself talking on the phone. I went numb and my voice sounded muffled. I thought, "No, it's not possible. They made a mistake. No that couldn't have happened!"

Sadly, it wasn't a mistake. Nearly half of my family was gone just like that. My sister, who I had never been alive without, was gone. Suzette loved all kinds of music. She loved anything Irish because of our heritage and was actually learning to speak Gaelic. She loved to read and also loved to cross-stitch all kinds of different things because she found it relaxing. We would no longer be able to talk about any of those things and wouldn't go to any more concerts together or even out to dinner. Suzette and all of that was gone and I was shattered into a million pieces.

I found out the details of the accident later. My sister was driving back to my parents' house and was about three miles from the exit when a deer jumped onto the interstate; they were nearly home. Suzette slowed to avoid hitting the deer and then changed lanes, but then realized there was a second deer in that lane. A tractor trailer was just a little ways behind them and with the heavy load it was carrying, it couldn't stop. The place it happened was close to an overpass and there was no shoulder for the truck to pull onto. The truck hit their car, the car that carried such precious cargo and forty-one-year-old Suzette, eight-year-old Lillian and six-year-old Vivian were gone instantly. There are still no words to describe the intense feeling of loss...loss of them, the joy they brought, the future with them, things we thought were meant to be, the loss of the life I knew, and the loss of myself. I didn't realize what grief was really like until this. Suzette and the girls have now been in heaven for three years and the rest of us have been in California for just over two. We are physically settled in, but are still trying to figure out this new life.

Without a doubt, I know where my sister and nieces are. But I still grieve for them. I miss them more than words can describe. Before losing them, I had lost all of my grandparents, other relatives, a few friends and acquaintances. Although those losses hurt and I cried for each one, none of them came close to the deep soul-searing pain and life changing experience of losing Suzette, Lillian, and Vivian. The life I had is gone. I died and was reborn a different person the day they moved to heaven.

It is still beyond comprehension that this happened. People say they don't know how we can deal with it; if I was on the outside, I would think the same. Some days the grief is so great that I do actually feel that way, but deep down I know that God is the main answer and banding together even closer as a family is the second.

*

MICHAEL SMITH
Michael's 39-year-old brother Patrick
was killed by an impaired driver in 2007

Patrick was an engaging, humorous, outgoing personality who loved his son, Dakota, more than anything. I always knew my brother was a giving person, but I didn't quite understand how many others felt the same way about him until his wake. More than three hundred people lined up on a cold December night to pay respect to him. It was this caring that kept him busy outside of his job at Gerber Scientific, picking up Dakota from his mother's house and later dropping him off. My brother had a hectic schedule and somehow managed to keep everything in order even though he didn't have nearly enough time to himself. He was driving on Route 74 on his way to work from Mansfield, Connecticut. He was at an intersection, probably running the day's schedule through his mind while waiting for the light to turn green. Coming north on Route 32, an impaired diabetic driver sped through a red light and crashed into the side of Patrick's Saturn sedan, the force pushing his car diagonally across the street. Patrick's seat was literally pushed onto the passenger seat. He suffered massive internal injuries, but was not killed instantly. Eyewitnesses said he was breathing for several minutes before the medics arrived. My day started at 7 a.m. with that phone call from my father.

*

DAWN WOINOVICK
Dawn's 52-year-old brother
Todd died from cancer in 2013

My brother Todd was a badass. Yes, he lived a hard life. When he finally wanted to live right, it turned out that his days were numbered. Todd was a great brother and friend. We grew up like twins, doing everything together. At least until his friends started asking me out, a little bump in the road and we parted ways for a time. I moved to Alaska; he stayed in Pennsylvania. Then one day Todd called and said he wanted to straighten out his life and come see his niece and nephew, because by then I had started a family. Well, Todd met a girl who wasn't so good. I moved back to Pennsylvania, and he stayed in Alaska. Years later all of us wound up here in Pennsylvania.

Todd was diagnosed with cancer and spent four years fighting the good fight. I helped him get his heart right and ask for forgiveness. But his death wasn't peaceful. Hospice dropped the ball and on his last day and a half, Todd cried and moaned. Hospice finally came to give him a shot and less than ten hours later I watched my brother take his last breath.

I miss my brother dearly, and my heart still aches for my brother, my friend, and the boy and man who knew me better than anyone. Now I just look forward to the day I cross over to see him.

CHAPTER TWO

THE AFTERMATH

Somehow, even in the worst of times, the tiniest fragments of good survive. It was the grip in which one held those fragments that counted. -MELINA MARCHETTA

Following profound loss, the first questions we often ask ourselves are: How am I going to survive this? How can I function when I have no feeling or when those sensations are so strong they threaten to paralyze me? How can I cook and clean and cope? There we stand in the aftermath, feeling vulnerable and often ravaged with fear. How do we survive?

*

EMILY BAIRD-LEVINE
Emily's 43-year-old brother Don
died from a heart attack in 2004

The first few weeks were very difficult. I remember not being able to sleep, eat, or focus clearly on anything. It was a nightmare. I became more of a homebody than previously. If I did go out, it needed to be brief or I would begin to panic. I just wanted to be safely at home.

I was so fortunate to be able to talk to my sister, Nicki, on a regular basis even though we live in different states. I believe that Don helped us get through this time. He would click the phone whenever I was talking on the phone with my sister or with his fiancée, Kitty. He would also click the phone when I was on the phone with someone who wasn't especially supportive or understanding of my loss. Don seemed to be conveying that he was still here, and we were going to be all right without him. It was a comfort. I was sad when the clicking stopped. It probably lasted about a year, if I recall correctly.

Even though I was never an observant Jew, my family used to at least have a nice, special Shabbat meal on Friday nights. We would light candles, say blessings, and eat. When Don died, I couldn't bring myself to do any of these things anymore. This lasted years. I simply couldn't find the joy in it any longer or the motivation and effort to make this happen. I really spent a lot of time breaking into tears and getting hugs from my husband, Bob, and trying somehow to make sense of the whole thing.

When Don had his kidney transplant (we were blessed that my eldest brother, Andy, donated the kidney), we were told that the kidney would last for ten years. Don lived twenty-four years after the transplant. So, knowing all along that Don's health wouldn't hold up was constantly in the back of my head. Every time he got sick, it was scary not knowing what would come of it. Would he pull through? He was such a trooper; so strong, a fighter. Somehow I believed he would pull through and live a long life.

I believe that part of my coping was remembering what is important in this life and attempting to not worry about the little things. I have never been the best at this, but I did strive to do so. My kids were almost nine and almost eleven when their Uncle

Donald died. They both knew him and had fond memories of him. As a result, they learned at an early age what is truly important. Whenever they complained about anything of little significance I would ask them, "What is really important?" They both would answer, "Losing Uncle Donald." or "You losing your brother." This really kept things in perspective, harsh as it may seem.

I tried my best during the first few months to stay in some sort of routine. I was always active helping out at my kids' elementary school and on the swim team my youngest was already on. So, I continued to do so. I got busy on the PTA board and tried to contribute as best as I could. It wasn't easy and I often found that people didn't understand what I was going through and didn't quite know how to relate to me, my grief, or when I mentioned my brother in any way. This was isolating.

*

CHRISTINE BASTONE
Christine's 38-year-old sister
Liz died by suicide in 2012

That first night I went online and searched for how to deal with this tragedy that had happened. I also joined two Yahoo groups. I was very, very busy for about the next two weeks. I wasn't deliberately busy, that's usually just the nature of death I think. But I believe that it did help.

There was discussion about whether or not we would go to the memorial service. There was packing, and making all the arrangements to be out of town for a few days. There was the long two-day drive up to Ohio from Florida, and then there was getting situated in our motel room once we got there. There was seeing my sister's body, saying what I wanted to say to her, and watching my mother's anguish over the loss of her youngest child...her baby.

33

There was helping to write Liz's online obituary for the funeral home's website. There was going to the florist, and helping to pick out flowers for my sister. There was going to the cemetery where she would be buried. There was helping to pick out her tombstone.

Since we ended up being there a few more days than we expected, I even got to do a few things that I had been wanting to do for a while such as going to a lake that I used to live right across from. There was meeting old friends at church. There was writing my first, and so far only, eulogy. There was getting ready for the memorial service. There was the memorial service, and the get-together afterward. There was visiting with my dad's sister, and catching up with her. And before I knew it, there was the very long drive home.

Like I said, I was busy! But I was okay. My appetite was a little off, and I couldn't sleep for more than four hours a night, but otherwise I think I handled it well. As is normal in such situations, we had a lot of support during those first few weeks. And of course I was also still in shock. So it wasn't until I got back home again and it felt like everyone had disappeared that things got a lot tougher to handle, and when my grief really began.

*

SHANNON BOOS
Shannon's 21-year-old brother Kevin
was killed by two drunk drivers in 2015

I like the wording of this question, because a lot of people who ask me this ask how I lived in the first few months. I didn't live. I was surviving. Every single day was making sure I was breathing, and that I still had blood pumping through my body. It sure didn't feel like I was alive, but I guess I was.

I had spent two years at Florida State with Kevin, and had earned my associate's degree. I worked really hard and was accepted into the Elementary Education program at the University of Florida in Gainesville, the best program in the state.

Before Kevin was killed, I was an atypical (A-typical) twenty-year-old college girl. All I did was work out, go to school, study, work out some more, and was always productive in some way. I would like to go out with my friends sometimes too, but I wasn't one to really sit still, especially when there were things to do. I had just started classes and was at the top of my game, on top of the world, and so happy at my new school.

That night Kevin was killed, every single thing about me changed. I did nothing. And I am not exaggerating when I use the word "nothing." My family's dog, Nala, was living with me in my apartment, and to this day I believe she is one of the only reasons I am still alive. She made me get out of bed to walk her, feed her, etc. But that was the only time I really would get up. I would typically wake up hungover, vomit a couple of times, and crawl right back into bed. I'd get up to walk Nala whenever she needed to go outside, but besides that I hid under my covers with the lights off.

Then 7 p.m. would hit, and I saw this as an acceptable time to start drinking. That is when I would start my one or two bottles of wine, and drink until I couldn't see straight.

I can remember back in 2013, when I was a freshman in college and Kevin had his own "cool" apartment with a few of his friends and they would throw parties all the time. I would of course attend and bring friends, and it was always a night to remember.

However, there was one night when I drank way too much, trying to cover up a heartbreak that I was going through. I remember vomiting in Kevin's bathroom, bawling my eyes out and screaming for him. He came running, and didn't leave my side the whole night, even while I was throwing up and inconsolable. His friends had all left the apartment to go to a club, but he stayed with me. He was there.

Two years later I found myself in the bathroom, drunk beyond belief, vomiting, and hysterically crying. But this time I would lie on the cold tile floor alone, and no matter how many times I would scream his name, he wouldn't come. And every single time the roaring silence would rip a bigger hole into my chest.

I didn't live after he was killed. But I did survive. And to this day, I truly cannot tell you how.

*

LISA FORESTBIRD
Lisa's 40-year-old brother Rob died
from a pontine hemorrhage in 2006

Luckily I was living with my mom and dad and I think that made it easier. I was thirty-nine years old but after two weeks of travel, the first night back home both my mom and dad tucked me into bed and that was very comforting.

My mom insisted I jump right back to work so as not to wallow in self-pity. So I worked and went about my activities of daily living. I did allow myself frequent cry breaks and my internal rule was Rob was worth it. I would cry anytime, anywhere, and for as long and intensely as I needed to. Every cry was the chance to tell a stranger about Rob, if I happened to be in the company of strangers and they happened to ask. Also, Rob's dog was left an orphan because his girlfriend could not handle Winston. Caring for Winston brought me great comfort and joy.

*

BONNIE FORSHEY
Bonnie's 54-year-old sister Eunice
died from bladder cancer in 2010

The loss of my sister was very difficult. She was my best friend and we had been there for one another since birth. It was a huge loss and I felt so alone. Eunice died of cancer, and I watched her suffer immensely. I was glad that she was out of her misery, but it was only beginning for me. I cried a lot, but had to be strong for her three children.

*

LAURA HABEDANK
Laura's brother Brian died
by suicide in 2010 at age 35

It doesn't feel appropriate to say I was in "shock" because to be honest, I wasn't all that surprised that my brother ended his own life. But I just felt completely numb. I spent the next few months in a complete fog. I couldn't sleep through the night, I didn't feel like eating, I was experiencing racing thoughts of guilt and panic, and I felt physically ill most of the time. My own existing depression was shoved into high gear, and I responded by drinking too much, not answering my phone for anyone but my mom, and I recall endless hours lying on my right side, on my bed, and staring up at the silhouette of the trees outside my window against the bright blue sky and being so confused as to how it could look so beautiful out there and how the world seemed to keep moving on without me when I felt so exceedingly empty inside.

I spent so much time going over each and every detail of our last conversations and interactions, as if searching for a way to go back and get a "do-over," and possibly reach a different outcome. I was tormenting myself over all of the what ifs and the if onlys that my mind was a constant windstorm of self-doubt and self-blame for my brother's decision. I was obsessed with finding answers that in fact would never be found. I tried desperately to gain access to his cellphone, email and other account passwords, thinking, if only I could just see the last email he ever sent... or the last text he ever sent or received... or find out how he was able to obtain the illegal substances he ingested that resulted in his death then perhaps I'd be able to get some of the answers that I so desperately needed. I knew that the answers to those questions wouldn't bring my brother back, but I foolishly thought that they might bring me some comfort. In the end, all the frustratingly fruitless searching only left a bigger hole in my heart.

I became obsessed with researching details that could only serve to bring more pain to myself, such as endlessly combing the internet for pictures and details about decomposition and the substances that would later be revealed to have been found in Brian's system. I wanted to know what he looked like when they found him. I needed to know who out there contributed to his death by either selling him those controlled substances or by posting the instructions online that describe the correct amounts to use, the correct combination to use, and in what order to ingest them. It took me a very long time to realize that, in the end, no one else was responsible for it. If it hadn't been this way, Brian would have found another way to do it. I just hoped that he didn't experience a great deal of physical pain.

I withdrew from the world. I did what I had to do to get by, such as getting myself to work and all, but I felt absolutely nothing; no connection to anyone. It felt pointless, really. No one could possibly understand the magnitude of the agony I was experiencing, so why bother? I had absolutely no patience for the seemingly trivial things going on with those around me. Hearing a coworker complain how life sucked so much because his or her car was in the shop was just more than I could handle. I was always on the verge of telling everyone around me, "My brother just killed himself!!! I'll tell you how much life sucks."

Friends expressed their desire to have the "old Laura" back. That really hurt. I knew the "old me" wasn't ever coming back; you can't experience a loss of that magnitude and not be irreversibly changed. I wanted to know that I would still be loved, accepted and supported even in the new, broken form I was taking because I knew that from then on I would never, ever be the same.

*

MARCELLA MALONE
Marcella's 20-year-old brother
Michael died by suicide in 2014

The initial aftermath was a giant mix of shock, pain, and questions. I stayed with my parents from the night it happened until the day following the funeral. A week full of planning, chaos, meeting with detectives because of the gunshot, accusations, and lots of love. That last part got me through it. The love I had for my unborn child helped me take care of myself and stay calm, because he deserved that. The love of the countless family and friends who traveled to spend the days with us and make sure we didn't have to worry about things like food and cleaning made it easier to get by each moment.

The most important lives were those of my parents and my older brother and his fiancée who were also expecting their first child. We had to work together and take care of one another as we learned how to accept the shocking reality that Michael was really gone. The simplicity of having someone to sit with me so I wasn't alone in my grief was the most powerful. Nothing anyone said could have helped. Their just being there like a rock was the best. It is a time when you really find out who is there for you.

As the week progressed, it also helped to share stories about the amazing young man Michael was with family and friends. Memories were all we had left so we had to cherish them. When I returned home, it was more difficult to remember to take care of myself. I focused on the arrival of my child in July to keep my mind off the heartache. When I did break down, I was lucky to have an amazing roommate to comfort me through my nightmares, as well as my boyfriend to talk to me when I needed it. I also found it very helpful to remain close with Michael's good friends, as it helped keep his spirit alive for me.

At the end of each day I'm still learning to cope. It's an evolving process.

*

BROOKE NINNI MATTHEWS
Brooke's 31-year-old brother Timothy
died by homicide in 2012

The morning I received the call telling me my brother had been murdered, my heart sank, my stomach did twirls, and my body was numb! I remember vomiting, screaming and not being able to catch my breath. Several hours later I was still not able to catch my breath, so I was rushed to the ER where they told me I was having an anxiety attack. They sent me home with anxiety medication and advised me to see a psychologist.

I saw a psychologist for a few months and it helped me get through for a while, but I still had thoughts of suicide because I just could not bear the pain of losing my brother like I did. I slowly worked myself through the emotions and pain and took his clothes and made a beautiful memory quilt with them, which was very therapeutic.

Our family had to relive that morning for months afterward, because of hearings and trials for the perpetrator. When all the hearings and trials are over, you always hear others say, "Well, at least you have closure now." Words of advice: there is never any closure. A homicide victim's family serves a sentence long after the perpetrator's sentence is over.

*

NICKI NOBLE
Nicki's 43-year-old brother Don
died from a heart attack in 2004

Survive? I was in a fog for quite a long time. I cried often. I looked at pictures and talked about my brother to anyone who would listen. I tried to remember the funny things he always did. I was fortunate to have a very supportive husband and friends. It was difficult for my siblings and I, because we were all grieving.

*

MARYELLEN ROACH
MaryEllen's 41-year-old sister Suzette
died in a car accident in 2012

There is a large chunk of time after the accident that is still a blur. When I do remember things, I have no idea about when it happened. I remember that right after my mom called to tell me the news, I called my best friend Leah to tell her what happened. She started crying hysterically, but as we sat on the phone together, I was completely calm and almost confused by her reaction. Leah could tell I was in deep shock and shouldn't drive myself to my parents' house, so she drove the hour between her house and mine to take me to my parents' house, which was another hour away.

While I was waiting for her to arrive at my house, I stood in my bedroom trying to figure out what I needed to do. I stared at my clothes for what seemed like an eternity, while trying to get my head together enough to pack. I remember thinking, "Oh, my God. I have to take clothes for the visitation and funeral." The thought of that was beyond horrible and so unreal. Somehow I finally got my clothes together. I barely remember the drive, but I do remember that I knew exactly where the accident happened even without anyone telling me. I'm still not sure how, because it was so dark that the skid marks couldn't be seen.

I went with my parents to plan the visitation and funeral, but I was so numb I mostly just stared at the carpet. Thank God my parents had enough of their wits about them to get everything planned. I remember wanting to see my sister and nieces' bodies, but the funeral director denied my request because they weren't ready to be seen. I was concerned they wouldn't do a good job with Suzette's makeup and I wanted to do it myself, but then realized that was an insane thought, because there was no way I could have handled it.

The visitation and seeing the bodies in the caskets for the first time was absolutely horrible and I literally thought I would die. I already felt like I was in a nightmare I couldn't wake up from. And seeing three caskets with the bodies of Suzette, Lillian, and Vivian seemed so unreal especially since they didn't look like them anymore. Several hundred people came to the visitation, including my manager at the time, friends I had worked with for years, and even a couple of people whom I had only worked with for a short time, which meant a lot.

A couple of days after the funeral, we all began going through their things. This was incredibly difficult, but now I realize it was a blessing to have gone through it all while the shock was still so prominent. I took two weeks off from work and thought going back would help me get through it all. I was completely mistaken and it took a couple of months for me to realize I couldn't force my mind to stay on task. Thoughts always went back to what happened and wondering how I could continue life without them. I made an appointment with our family doctor and after talking to him for a few minutes, I was advised to stop working immediately and begin counseling. I also began staying with my parents because it made it a little easier being together. I don't remember much from my counseling sessions, but I do remember being told to stay hydrated and be overly kind to myself; which was great advice. I also remember being given official diagnoses that included posttraumatic stress disorder. I was initially confused because I thought only soldiers got PTSD after being in traumatic combat, but the symptoms completely fit me.

I hated going to counseling because that meant I had to shower and get dressed, which I didn't care a thing about. I hated having to go back to my house, because Suzette's room (the second bedroom in my house) smelled like her. I closed the door to her room and pretended she was in there sleeping. I don't remember much else after the accident; most of that time was spent sitting in a chair being completely numb, and my mom making my dad and I eat. To this day I don't know how my mom kept herself collected enough to take care of us. I know I prayed a lot during that time, prayed for strength one minute and prayed to die the next. It was the darkest time in my life. When I think back on it, it's like my memories of that time literally have a dark cloud or shadow over them. I only got through it with the help of God and my family.

*

MICHAEL SMITH
Michael's 39-year-old brother Patrick
was killed by an impaired driver in 2007

I went into anger mode, searching nonstop for days to find similar incidents and for ways to have the other driver punished. I stayed in anger mode for a very long time.

*

DAWN WOINOVICK
Dawn's 52-year-old brother
Todd died from cancer in 2013

Barely, I felt very alone. Like there was nothing anywhere to give me any support as a sibling. So I just took my pain, tucked it away and went about helping my folks and others just busying myself. When a thought would come up I would walk away to cry, get my Bible, pray or just talk to Todd. As time went on I would find little things here and there for siblings, but I feel there is really not enough especially since siblings spend so much time together and are interconnected on so many different levels

*

CHAPTER THREE

THE FUNERAL

The song has ended, but the melody lingers on.
-IRVING BERLIN

For many the funeral represents the end while for others it marks the beginning of something eternal. Regardless of whether we mourn the absence of our sibling's physical body or celebrate the spirit that continues on, planning the funeral or memorial service presents emotionally-laden challenges shared by many.

*

EMILY BAIRD-LEVINE
Emily's 43-year-old brother Don
died from a heart attack in 2004

Don was cremated and the ashes were given to his fiancée, Kitty. Don had so many friends who loved him. They planned a memorial service for him a few weeks after he passed away. It was at Pomona College where he went to school. A rabbi from the college led a short reform Jewish service. Several people spoke at the service including Kitty, Don's good friend, Brian, and my eldest brother Andy. I wasn't able to speak but my sister and I stood up with Andy when he spoke. A friend of Don's sang a beautiful song, as well. There were lots of family and friends there from all the different parts of Don's life. Friends from growing up, high school friends, college friends, coworkers, old family friends, teachers, and relatives were there. Our parents had already passed away.

The service was followed by a party in celebration of Don's life. There was a lot of food and drink. A PowerPoint of Don's escapades doing fun activities like bungee jumping, sky diving, and just being his silly, fun, outgoing, "live life to the fullest" self was playing on repeat for everyone to enjoy and remember. There were little pictures for everyone to take home of Don, along with small and colorful rubber ducks. I didn't really participate in the planning of the memorial. We let Don's friends and fiancée plan what was appropriately called, "Don, The Party." The only one physically missing was Don. He would have had a great time at his party.

*

CHRISTINE BASTONE
Christine's 38-year-old sister
Liz died by suicide in 2012

My sister Pam, her husband Paul, and Liz's husband Adam planned the memorial service. Since I didn't help plan it, I don't know too many of the details. As far as I know, almost everything went smoothly. Or at least as smoothly as could be expected.

The only real problem that I know about is that they had a really hard time finding a minister who was willing to speak at the service. Once they found out that Liz had died by suicide, all of them refused.

I believe it was a friend of Pam and Paul's who was the minister who ended up speaking. And he was out of town at the time the service was being planned. We had to wait for him to come back in town before we could have the service. This is why we ended up being out of town longer than we had anticipated.

I wasn't there when this was happening. I found out about it about two days before the service. This upset me to no end! How dare they refuse! This only hurts and punishes the family that is left behind. It is not right. Even if Liz deserved that, and I absolutely don't believe that she did, we certainly didn't.

Except for the ministers who refused to speak, everybody involved really did an awesome job at planning my sister's memorial service.

Liz's memorial service was very nice. The only things I wish could have been different were that I wasn't ready for it to end, I wish more people would have been there, and that more could have stayed for the get-together afterward. I got there a half hour early. They were playing a very nice DVD that had a bunch of pictures of Liz with beautiful music playing in the background. I started watching it, and that was the only time that tears came to my eyes that day. It seems that I can cry at anything but funerals and memorial services!

Before it was over, people started coming in. I stopped watching (but got my own copy later), and went to greet them. I was a real social butterfly that day, which is so not like me. I saw people who I hadn't seen in years. That part was nice. Then the service started. It was basically the minister speaking, and then the three eulogies.

It's kind of funny, for once I wasn't nervous. Public speaking always makes me nervous, but not that day. Of course I did write out what I was going to say ahead of time, so all I had to do was read it. It was also pretty short. But I think that I did a good job, and

I felt like I connected with the audience...so I'm proud of that very important speech. I was also proud of how well my mother and Pam did as well. And I am happy to say that I have a copy of all of our words to always remember. After it was over, people came up to talk to us for just a minute, sort of like a receiving line at a wedding. And then we went to a nearby church for a get-together. A number of people couldn't stay for that. That was disappointing, but I understood. Especially as some of the people only had a day or two of notice. It was so nice of them to come at all. Again I was a social butterfly. I didn't really sit down and eat until I was done talking to everyone.

Then we went to Pam's house. My Aunt Barbara, my dad's only sister, came too. We sat down on the couch and talked for a while. She showed us pictures of her kids, my cousins, and their families, and told us all about what was going on with them. I hadn't seen her in I don't know how long, so it was nice to catch up with her. We couldn't stay too late because we were leaving first thing the following morning. So we said our goodbyes and went back to our motel room. It's certainly a day that I will never forget.

*

SHANNON BOOS
Shannon's 21-year-old brother Kevin
was killed by two drunk drivers in 2015

My entire family worked together to plan the funeral, and I really don't know how we could have done it otherwise. When one person was weak, everyone else was strong. We held each other together.

We wanted to make sure that the funeral was as "Kevin" as it could get. We had Miami Dolphins themed "tickets" that we gave to people who attended. We provided baskets full of Pop-Tarts

48

(chocolate chip and wild berry, of course), and Goldfish, his favorite snacks. My other brother, my mom, my dad, other friends, and I all wrote speeches from the heart, but added a little bit of humor, because that's what he would have wanted.

However, that week was undoubtedly horrible, mostly because we also lost Vincenzo and Morgan, so there were two other burials, funerals, viewings, ceremonies, etc. to attend in the time of our own grief. It was easily the most exhausting and overwhelming week of my life.

I still remember seeing his body in the casket for the first time. We had a private family viewing, and I remember waiting to go into the room where he was, and asking my dad if I could give him a kiss, not sure if I was allowed to touch him. He told me I could, but warned me that it would be shocking to feel his cold, stiff skin. I told him I was prepared, and we went into the room.

There is so much from that week that I do not remember; everything is so blurry. But it scares me how well I remember walking in to see him for the first time. I was taken aback, because I was able to see him from the doorway and I guess I hadn't fully prepared myself. My heart fell into my stomach and I stopped in my tracks. Then again, who could ever fully prepare to see their twenty-one-year-old brother dead in a casket?

I walked in, holding my mother's and grandmother's hands. My mother walked up with tears on her face, looked at him, and walked away. I looked at him, and leaned in and gave him a kiss on the forehead. And instantly regretted it.

To this day, I still can't press a cold drink to my lips without getting flashbacks of his frozen forehead touching my lips.

I froze. I couldn't move. I couldn't take my gaze off him.

"This isn't him. This isn't him! There's no way. Maybe he's just asleep. He has to be asleep. He looks like he is just sleeping. Why is there makeup on his face? Those aren't his real freckles. When is he going to wake up? Kevin, wake up! Kevin, please wake up. Please. Please wake up."

He didn't wake up.

During the entire ceremony I would look over at him. Waiting for him to move. Waiting for him to wake up and tell us he had just pulled off the biggest prank of the century.

Today, I still can't watch my boyfriend while he is asleep next to me, because it reminds me of my brother's unmoving, dead body. I was diagnosed with PTSD after all of the trauma I went through, mostly being affected by seeing Kevin in a casket. I fear that I will not even be able to watch my future children sleep. How could something so beautiful and so peaceful bring me such terrible, traumatizing memories?

It shouldn't be this way.

*

LISA FORESTBIRD
Lisa's 40-year-old brother Rob died
from a pontine hemorrhage in 2006

Mostly my mom handled the funeral arrangements but I was involved, as was my dad and little brother. We ended up having two funerals. Jim did the eulogy at one, and I did the other. I think we disagreed over minor things but for better or worse, when Rob lay in his hospital bed for six days in his coma, we made a pact, willingly or not, to stick together and not disagree on major things.

*

BONNIE FORSHEY
Bonnie's 54-year-old sister Eunice
died from bladder cancer in 2010

My niece and nephews decided on cremation. We had a small service. I made a DVD of her life in pictures, and it was very nice.

*

LAURA HABEDANK
Laura's brother Brian died
by suicide in 2010 at age 35

Having a mother who has worked in a funeral home for as far back as I can recall, I was not at all unfamiliar with the subject of death, funerals or the details that go into planning one. It was all pretty much second nature to me, as I had grown so comfortable with all of it over the years. But accepting the fact that it was now a funeral for my one and only sibling was just unbearable. Nothing about it felt real.

I told my mom that I wanted the opportunity to see my brother's body because I absolutely needed that closure for myself, if only to prove to myself that it was real. I had my mind set on going to the funeral home to view Brian's body. But I never had the chance. The funeral directors, whom I'd known for so many years and consider wonderful friends, came to the house to see me in person and tell me they didn't recommend my seeing him. I recall one of them basically saying to me, "We understand the immense importance of closure, and when at all possible, we give families the chance to see the body of the deceased, even if it means just being able to see a single hand and hold it one last time. I've known Brian for years but in all honesty, if I hadn't been told that it was him, there is no way I'd have recognized him at all. I think it would be detrimental to you to see him in that state and would cause you far more harm than you can imagine." I was devastated. My mind was a blur and my imagination ran absolutely wild. I couldn't control the thoughts racing in my head about how bad Brian must have looked to have been told I couldn't even see a hand or a foot to be able to have that tangible proof for myself. I kept thinking that maybe I should see him because surely the things I'm imagining in my head have to be far worse than reality, you know? They did take some photos at my request, in case somewhere down the road I change my mind and still feel I need to see them for closure. To be honest, five years later I still have not ruled out asking to see those photos, because I still experience days where a rogue thought gets hold of me and I think, "Maybe this is all just a bad dream. I never did actually see him, so how do I know it was really him?"

For the most part, my mom took care of the details of the funeral. Brian, in his letter to us, had chosen cremation for himself so that's what we did. He wasn't a religious person, nor am I, so we held the service at the funeral home, not in a church. I chose the writings to be included in the funeral program, and my mom and I picked out the songs to be performed together.

The funeral itself was surreal. If only Brian could have seen how deeply he was loved and appreciated — the sheer number of people who showed up to celebrate his life was staggering. I recall one specific moment of the funeral, during one of the songs, when I took a look around the room and felt an overwhelming rush of peace and love as I looked at the sea of faces all there to support me and my family; it's so hard to put into words, but it's as though I felt a collective set of imaginary arms holding me in a warm embrace to let me know I wasn't alone in my grief. It was both heartbreaking and beautiful. It's a moment that has remained as vivid in my memory as the day it happened. I'm so grateful for that.

*

MARCELLA MALONE
Marcella's 20-year-old brother
Michael died by suicide in 2014

Less than twenty-four hours after being notified that Michael had taken his life, we were overwhelmed with questions about when the funeral would be. My mom just opened the phonebook and called the first funeral home listed. Twelve hours later, my mom, dad, older brother and his fiancée, and I sat in a room waiting to do the unimaginable. No one had seen this coming, and we struggled to comprehend the reality enough to make decisions. We all wanted it over with. We chose to have Michael cremated, as my parents wanted to be able to bury him with them. So we had just a simple ceremony at the funeral home. Our friends and family arranged a lunch at our house following it; they were amazing.

No urn seemed fit. It wasn't where Michael, so young, belonged. We chose to have his ashes placed in a football. It truly seemed fitting, and was beautiful. The hardest part was probably seeing the obituary in the paper. That's when it really hit home for us that Michael was actually gone.

On April 19, just five days after Michael's death, we prepared for a truly hard day. We lined up at the entrance and everyone offered their love and condolences. Nothing they said seemed right to me and it took everything I had to stay strong. As we moved into the room we had Michael's amazing football coaches as pastors, and his pictures and favorite thing surrounded us. All the seats were filled and people were left standing. The love for Michael was powerful and huge. I just wish he could have seen it.

I couldn't leave quick enough when it was over. I was done. That wasn't him. As we returned to our house everything was more relaxed and we honored Michael with food and a party and lots of memory sharing. No drama. That was him and what he deserved. The longest week of my life was over.

*

BROOKE NINNI MATTHEWS
Brooke's 31-year-old brother Timothy
died by homicide in 2012

My dad, sisters, and I had Timothy cremated and divided his ashes among us. We had a memorial for him in the church our aunt belonged to at the time. It was a very emotional memorial and there were three hundred-plus people in attendance. People were standing out in the church lobby because there weren't enough seats for everyone. My brother was well known and loved in our community where we grew up.

*

NICKI NOBLE
Nicki's 43-year-old brother Don
died from a heart attack in 2004

My sweet brother was cremated. We had a large memorial at his college alumni house. The event was planned primarily by his fiancée and his friends. My family was in such a fog, if there were any problems, I was not aware. My brother loved the short life he had, so this event was more of a celebration of life then a serious sad event. There was a PowerPoint presentation and my older brother spoke, as did Don's fiancée. That was something I was not able to do. There were no disagreements that I was aware of. Many childhood friends came as well as family friends from our childhood and relatives from the East Coast.

*

MARYELLEN ROACH
MaryEllen's 41-year-old sister Suzette
died in a car accident in 2012

I went with my parents to plan the visitation and funeral, but I was so numb I didn't take part in most of it. I mostly remember just staring at the carpet, but I did help pick out Suzette's casket and urn for her ashes. Thank God my parents had enough of their wits about them to get everything planned. The funeral director asked for pictures so they could make a slideshow that would play during the visitation. I was tasked with getting those together and thankfully I could still handle looking at pictures at that time.

The first time I saw their bodies was the day of the visitation, which was Sunday, July 29. It was absolutely horrible and I literally thought I would die when I saw them. It was so completely overwhelming that my mind couldn't process it all. I already felt like I was in a nightmare I couldn't wake up from, and seeing three caskets with the bodies of Suzette, Lillian and Vivian seemed so unreal, especially since the bodies I saw didn't really look like them. Suzette's hair and makeup were done and I was surprised at how well it had been done. I remember feeling relief, because I think Suzette would have been satisfied with it. I stood at the front of the room with my parents next to Suzette's casket, to greet everyone. Although I know the soul and body are two very different entities, at the time I thought it was bizarre how Suzette was right there, but I couldn't feel her. I feel almost silly that I thought that, but I realize it was my head still not accepting what happened.

Several hundred people came to the visitation, including my manager at the time, friends I had worked with for years, and even a couple of people who I had only worked with for a short time, management and coworkers from Suzette's job, college friends of

Suzette's, teachers and the principal from Lillian and Vivian's school as well as a few of their classmates. Suzette's coworkers all told us how much they loved Suzette, how nice she always was and how much they would miss her. Her friends from college were beside themselves, because they were all more than just friends, they became more like extended family. It meant more than I can explain that so many people came to pay their respects, say their goodbyes and support us. I think Suzette, Lillian, and Vivian would have been surprised to see how many people loved them so much.

The funeral was the next day, which was a Monday, and I was even less present that day. A lot of people attended the funeral as well, but much fewer than the visitation since it was a weekday. I don't remember much of what the preacher said during the funeral, but I remember being satisfied with his message. When the funeral was over, the lids on the caskets were closed and then rolled out of the church. As I watched that happen, I remember feeling emptiness and despair that went to my core and I remember thinking, "Oh, my god. That's the last time I'll ever see my sister!" I fell apart. It felt so utterly harsh and final and it was so hard to accept that was all there was. It still is.

*

MICHAEL SMITH
Michael's 39-year-old brother Patrick
was killed by an impaired driver in 2007

The funeral was planned by my parents. Patrick was buried in a public ceremony with his friends and coworkers joined by many friends of the family and by those whose lives had been touched by my brother. The receiving line went on for over three hours with over four hundred guests. I remember most of it. I felt very angry and protective of my family. I will never forget the feeling of flying home to San Diego afterward and just being stunned; it was all so surreal. It was then I realized that I wouldn't have another morning wake up to my brother calling me during his break at work around 10 a.m. Eastern time and me waking up at 7 a.m. Pacific time.

*

DAWN WOINOVICK
Dawn's 52-year-old brother
Todd died from cancer in 2013

My folks and I did get to be a part of the whole process. We have a very tight family, there was just the four of us. Sad only three now. We had a beautiful viewing, although I'm not a fan. I would rather hold my happy memories than have my last be not real, so to speak. We had a service at the grave and that was hard. When we picked flowers I made sure I got a special white rose, different from all the others, like somehow Todd would know it was from me. His stone is beautiful and unique, just like him. I visit often, sometimes with balloons with messages written on them sending my love on special days.

*

Long for me as I for you, forgetting what will be
inevitable, the long black aftermath of pain.

MALCOLM LOWRY

*

CHAPTER FOUR

THE TRANSITION

The bereaved need more than just the space to grieve the loss. They also need the space to grieve the transition. -LYNDA CHELDELIN FELL

As we begin the transition of facing life without our sister or brother, some find comfort by immediately returning to a familiar routine, while others find solitude a safe haven. Sometimes our own circumstances don't allow choices to ponder, and we simply follow where the path leads. But the one commonality we're all faced with is the starting point that marks the transition from our old life to the new. Where do we begin?

*

EMILY BAIRD-LEVINE
Emily's 43-year-old brother Don
died from a heart attack in 2004

My husband and my kids went back to work and school a few days after Don passed away. Being an at-home mom, I continued with my normal routine as best I could. The transition of returning to my old routine now that Don was no longer in this world was extremely difficult. It would never be the same. Don and I would talk often; he always knew what was happening in our family and what his niece and nephew were up to. I think the transition was easier for my husband and kids because their routines were so much more defined and all encompassing. I spent a lot of time at home by myself just trying to get through each day and function adequately enough to meet the needs of my family.

*

CHRISTINE BASTONE
Christine's 38-year-old sister
Liz died by suicide in 2012

I don't have a paying job; I'm a stay-at-home mom. We were out of town for about a week. So that's how long my husband took off of work, and also how long I pulled my kids out of school. The transition went smoothly for my husband and my kids. It was very hard those first few months for me to focus even on basic things such as getting my kids off to school, and making dinner every night. I focused on grieving pretty close to twenty-four hours a day at that point. Focusing on anything else was extremely difficult. I did the best I could but I was relieved when summer came, and I didn't have to get the kids to and from school for a few months.

*

SHANNON BOOS
Shannon's 21-year-old brother Kevin
was killed by two drunk drivers in 2015

My father and mother were both incredibly strong for my brother and me, and very supportive of every decision we made. Not just after Kevin died, but always. But I know how lucky I am to have such strong, involved parents, as it was much needed during this time.

They told both my brother Jeffrey and me that we could take our time. "Don't worry about work right now. Don't worry about school either. Take care of yourself, we will support you. Find what is going to help you the most. If working will help you, do it. If doing nothing will help you, do nothing."

I was the first one to leave our family after the funerals. I was home for about eight days, and then decided to just pack my stuff up and head back to school in Gainesville, Florida, before I changed my mind. I was convinced that if I just ripped the bandage off and threw myself back into the world, it would work. I was proven wrong very quickly.

My mother left a couple of days after I did and headed back to her home in northern Florida. Jeffrey, my brother, was already living in southern Florida, and returned to work around the same time the rest of us did. My dad stayed home with Jeffrey for another week or so and then headed back to work and to his home in Tucson, Arizona.

While I did return to Gainesville, I didn't actually return to life itself. I withdrew from my classes, and decided to enroll in one online class just to try to have some sort of responsibility, but even that proved to be too daunting with all the grief I had to deal with. Every day I sat at the computer to start an assignment. And every day I got nothing done. So I withdrew from that as well.

Next, I tried to get a job. I ended up quitting two days later, knowing I would get fired if I kept showing up late and calling out of my shifts. But grief is unforgiving, and the world has no mercy upon the bereaved.

I didn't really transition back into life. I made the mistake of diving head first back into the world, and my plan backfired.

I remember crying in my bed most days, but on other days I was silent, unmoving, and not really there. My bed saw me more than anyone else did. Friends had gone back to their lives, and I guess I was expected to get on with mine too. But I didn't know how to. I found it physically impossible to get out of bed. It felt like a boulder was sitting on my chest and I couldn't move, and I could barely breathe. I was a vulnerable soul in a queen-sized bed, and grief had swallowed me whole.

*

LISA FORESTBIRD
Lisa's 40-year-old brother Rob died
from a pontine hemorrhage in 2006

My mom insisted I jump right back to work so as not to wallow in self-pity. So I worked and went about my activities of daily living. I did allow myself frequent cry breaks, and my internal rule was that Rob was worth it.

*

BONNIE FORSHEY
Bonnie's 54-year-old sister Eunice
died from bladder cancer in 2010

This transition was not easy. We had to clean and remodel my sister's home in order to sell it. We sold off her belongings, and divided it between the children. All three children went their different ways, and life as we knew it was over. I miss her so much and think of her every day.

*

LAURA HABEDANK
Laura's brother Brian died
by suicide in 2010 at age 35

I had been at my new job only for thirty days when Brian died, so I had very little support at my new job; I really didn't know anyone there very well yet. I came back to work only eleven days after getting the news of Brian's death, so in only ten days I had flown home from Texas to Minnesota, helped plan his funeral, cleaned out his home of all his belongings, suffered through his funeral and the empty days afterward, and then flew back to Texas to get back to "real life" again.

I recall getting to work early that Monday, feeling sick to my stomach, as I knew I absolutely was not feeling even remotely ready to get back to reality. As I sat down to turn on my computer, my manager bounced past me with a huge smile and said, "Hey, Laura! Good morning!! How are you??" But I guess that was more of a rhetorical question anyway, as she kept walking and didn't stick around for an answer. My heart hit the floor. That was the kind of greeting you give someone who has just returned from vacation, not someone returning from the funeral of her only sibling who just died by suicide. I began to sob quietly at my desk, and thought how I had never felt so alone in my life. My pain wasn't acknowledged, and that hurt a great deal but I found out the hard way that people don't want to deal with things that make them uncomfortable, so they just don't.

For the most part, I was avoided completely by my new coworkers, and few people even looked me in the eye. Not a single person said so much as, "I'm sorry for your loss." It was one of the most lonely and alienating experiences of my life.

Having been at the job for only a month so far, I was still in training, and I found myself struggling in the most unimaginable way. Not only was I feeling depressed, lonely and suicidal, but I was desperately trying to take in loads of new information for which I was going to be responsible while I was suffering from a complete and total lack of focus. My mind was elsewhere, and I had loads of trouble trying to process the things I was being taught. Information was going in and right back out again, so on top of feeling sad I was also feeling panicked that I was going to be fired because I just wasn't "catching on" and wasn't pulling my weight on the team. I absolutely dreaded going into work each day, and usually all the way to work, during my bathroom breaks, during my lunch hour, and on the drive home. For the most part I was able to hold back the tears when others were watching. But, there were times when I just didn't care who saw me crying, because it didn't really matter... it's not as though anyone seemed to care, anyway. You can cry all you want when you're invisible.

A month after the funeral, the manager at the company I'd left for this new job contacted me and asked if I would come back to work for them. She heard from a friend that I was struggling, and she offered me the chance to come back to work and again be surrounded by people who cared for me. I jumped at the chance. I'm still there five years later, and honestly, I'm grateful for that gesture every single day. The magnitude and importance of what that did for me is not lost on me. Everyone here welcomed me back with open arms and hugs and listening ears. Even if they didn't understand what I was going through, they cared enough to try.

*

MARCELLA MALONE
Marcella's 20-year-old brother
Michael died by suicide in 2014

Everyone returned to work and school at their own pace. It took my parents over a month, and it was still rough on them. My brother and his fiancée had to return to work the following week. For me, that week was the start of final papers and projects being turned in and/or presented and exams being taken. I had a lot to catch up on, and no choice but to return to school the Monday following the funeral.

It wasn't as easy as it sounded. I struggled to concentrate on anything other than what I had lost. I ended up failing half of my classes that semester. It was rough on me, and knocked me out of the running for future grad school plans. Little did I know at the time that I would find a much better fit shortly after, a field that could help other kids from making the same decision my brother did. My boss was very understanding and told me to come back to work when I was ready.

It was hard on me having free time to sit at home and think about the past and future. I ended up returning to work that Friday. My coworkers were great about working with me, to provide support and a break when I was having a weak moment. I will always be thankful for that.

*

BROOKE NINNI MATTHEWS
Brooke's 31-year-old brother Timothy
died by homicide in 2012

I do not work, so I didn't have to worry about returning to work. But my daughter had a really hard time wanting to go to school after the murder of my brother, her uncle.

*

NICKI NOBLE
Nicki's 43-year-old brother Don
died from a heart attack in 2004

I was a stay-at-home mom at the time. My husband and kids returned to work and school after the winter break. My sweet brother died on December 26. For me, the transition was a bit difficult. My circle of friends were supportive but until one goes through a loss, it is hard for others to understand. I was quite tearful for a long time. I also was the executor of Don's estate. I found it quite difficult to pay his bills, process the business end of his life. Lots of stress and tears. I remember saying to my husband that this wasn't right. My sweet brother should be alive and doing this mundane task. It was wrong that he was gone. He had so much more living to do.

*

BRIDGET PARK
Bridget's brother Austin died
by suicide in 2008 at age 14

I returned to school about three weeks after the suicide of my brother Austin. It was a few days before my thirteenth birthday. I purposely was late to my first class, and I will never forget walking into the classroom and everyone turning their heads toward me. Everyone knew my brother and was fully aware of what happened because we lived in a small town. Also, everyone from my school knew about my brother's suicide because my middle school and my brother's high school were joined together in one building.

I was extremely nervous to return to school because someone at my school started a rumor that I had gotten in a fight with Austin and then I shot him. That rumor hurt and disgusted me more than

I can ever put into words. But, when I returned to school, my peers were very sympathetic, thankfully, and the rumor never came up.

From then on out my peers were really supportive, but sometimes the way that they tried to support me had the opposite effect. Girls came forward saying that he was "like a brother to me," and it was very hurtful for me to hear that. I felt like people were acting like they knew my brother well so they could get attention from others, whereas I did everything in my power to seem somewhat stable and trying to hide my pain.

I stayed confined and only communicated with my two best friends when at school. I steered away from other students and friends because I knew that my presence made them uneasy. I felt like an animal in a glass box that everyone stared in awe at, like I was a rare species.

My school, however, was very supportive and more than willing to provide whatever tools necessary for me to catch up in school and to receive proper help. They were understanding when I skipped class to be alone and cry. They understood when I would get up and leave in the middle of class. But after I had my time alone, I would be called in to speak to the counselors. I was blessed to have such understanding teachers.

*

MICHAEL SMITH
Michael's 39-year-old brother Patrick
was killed by an impaired driver in 2007

I went back to work about two weeks after the accident. Coworkers and friends were supportive, but I was, and sometimes still am in a daze when I think about how it all happened. We were never contacted by the family or attorney of the man who struck

Patrick's car. I think that annoyed me the most. No flowers, nothing printed in the paper, no letter, nothing. From that point on I began to compile information about similar accidents and began to meet and communicate with families of similar crash victims. I stayed mad for a very long time, about five years, to be exact. On the eve of the five-year anniversary, which was also the closure on the statute of limitations in Connecticut, I had what was probably a breakdown. I opened a bottle of Stoli vodka and finished it. The very next morning I had a voicemail from Donna Gore that I didn't see from the evening before, asking if I would be interested in participating with one of her radio shows as Lady Justice.

*

DAWN WOINOVICK
Dawn's 52-year-old brother
Todd died from cancer in 2013

My folks are retired and I'm disabled so there basically has been a gradual transition back to a new normal. The new normal, well that's daily life without my brother. Life has changed drastically; we really don't do major holidays, none of us feel it. I'm sure in time that will change. Don't get me wrong, my children are grown. The youngest is twenty-one and is the only one that cares and I make sure I celebrate with her. I've tried to help Mom, I got her a voice thing and transferred my brother's voice greeting from his phone, so any of us can hear his voice anytime.

*

CHAPTER FIVE

THE QUESTION

Grievers use a very simple calendar. Before and after. -LYNDA CHELDELIN FELL

One day we have a sibling. The next, that brother or sister is no longer living. So where does this leave us when, inevitably, others ask how many siblings we have? How do we answer a question that appears simple to everyone but us?

*

EMILY BAIRD-LEVINE
Emily's 43-year-old brother Don
died from a heart attack in 2004

Usually when someone asks me how many siblings I have, I say that I have three siblings and one of them, my brother Don, passed away. This usually leads me to keep talking, feeling as if I need to explain further, fill in the silence. Or, with some people, I sense that they don't want to hear more. Often, people don't know what to say or seem uncomfortable with the subject altogether. I will adjust depending on what I'm picking up. Somewhere deep inside of me I feel as if, somehow if I keep talking and explaining, that either the outcome of my story will perhaps magically change (i.e., I wouldn't have actually lost my brother) or that the person listening would start to "get it" on some level. Perhaps they would share their own story of loss or of someone they know who has lost a sibling. Mostly, this doesn't happen. These conversations usually make me feel isolated, not understood, and awkward. I don't ever want to make people uncomfortable. At the same time, I hope for people to learn from my loss. What I mean is that I want people to remember what is important in this life because we don't know how much time any of us have. Ever since Don got really sick, I could see from the way he led his life that he was so aware that time was limited, and that it is imperative to make the most of life. I have tried to incorporate this into my life, succeeding some of the time. I truly want others to remember this too. Enjoy who is in your life now. You can't know when these people will be taken away. This sounds morbid. I don't mean it that way. We all need to be grateful for what we have and not take anything for granted.

*

CHRISTINE BASTONE
Christine's 38-year-old sister
Liz died by suicide in 2012

As I am in my forties, so the question doesn't really come up very often, if at all. Even so, I still consider myself as having two sisters. If asked, I would probably simply say that, unless I was asked for more details. Then I might say that I had two younger sisters...one who lives in Ohio, and one who died by suicide. I won't ever say that I have only one sister. That's just not an option for me! I do try to make it very clear who I am talking about though. It's my sister Pam who did this, and my sister Liz who did that. I also do the same with their husbands. It's Pam's husband Paul, and Liz's husband Adam...so it's clear who it is that I am talking about.

That's the part that has changed a little bit. But I will always consider myself to have, and say that I have, two sisters...just because one of them is no longer here in this physical world doesn't change that fact for me!

*

SHANNON BOOS
Shannon's 21-year-old brother Kevin
was killed by two drunk drivers in 2015

I hate this question. I really, really do. I have two brothers. Of course I do. I will always have two brothers. But how do you answer this question to an unsuspecting human being?

Typically, I am asked this question at doctor appointments. I did see a lot of doctors after Kevin was killed because I was dealing with so many mental health issues due to the trauma, and I was asked this question every time.

"Do you have any siblings?"

"Yes, I have two brothers."

"Are they in good health?"

"My brother Jeffrey is healthy. My brother Kevin was killed."

Silence.

"Oh. He was sick?"

"No. He was very healthy. He was murdered by a drunk driver."

"Oh. I'm so sorry."

And that was it. And that was always so upsetting to me. Because while my mind is now reeling, you expect me to answer health history questions about myself while I'm stuck on the thought that my brother is dead, and you don't really care.

It has been over a year since Kevin was killed, and this question still takes me aback. I always answered that I have two brothers. That will never change. I just hope that the person asking will be satisfied with that answer and move on to something else, especially if it is someone I am just meeting in passing.

Although I am not ashamed that my brother was killed, or embarrassed, I sometimes don't feel like talking about it. But then there are times that I want to be asked about it. I want to talk about him. I want to vent about how wrong this whole situation is, how hurt I am, how much I miss him. But no one really cares when it doesn't have to do with them. No one really knows what to say. So I just stay silent.

I still have two brothers; one is just my guardian angel now.

*

LISA FORESTBIRD
Lisa's 40-year-old brother Rob died
from a pontine hemorrhage in 2006

It depends. If I can slip it into conversation that I have two brothers, I do. For example, I might say one year for Christmas my brothers and I got space pens as that brings happy memories. If I'm referencing the present, such as stating my holiday plans, I may or may not reference my brother because it might make me and others sad. I can also feel angry or lonely when others talk about current interactions they are having with their siblings. I feel like I keep up a bit of a wall, even when I let others know my brother has passed away. That way I can still protect myself and reveal only as much of my raw emotions I am comfortable with.

*

BONNIE FORSHEY
Bonnie's 54-year-old sister Eunice
died from bladder cancer in 2010

I tell people that I had one sister and two brothers, but they are all deceased. I am all alone now.

*

MARCELLA MALONE
Marcella's 20-year-old brother
Michael died by suicide in 2014

When people ask me how many siblings I have, it so quickly rolls off my tongue that I have two brothers, one younger and one older. And then it hits that I only have one here. A year and a half later, I still struggle to believe Michael is really gone. When it hits, I immediately feel down and want to correct myself, as if I had said something wrong. Often times I follow up with mentioning that my younger brother passed away when he was twenty, dreading the possibility that the person I am talking to might ask more questions. I'm sure it will get easier, but at this point it has not.

*

BROOKE NINNI MATTHEWS
Brooke's 31-year-old brother Timothy
died by homicide in 2012

I have one older sister and three younger sisters.

*

NICKI NOBLE
Nicki's 43-year-old brother Don
died from a heart attack in 2004

I answer that I have a sister, a brother and a brother who passed away. It depends on the person asking and the situation. I don't always feel the need to explain about my deceased brother, so I might say that I have two brothers and a sister. The emotions that usually come to me are sadness and/or a good feeling because of my memories.

*

MARYELLEN ROACH
MaryEllen's 41-year-old sister Suzette
died in a car accident in 2012

I still answer with "two sisters." Suzette was my only biological sibling and I also have a younger adopted sister named Ashley. Suzette is still very much alive in heaven and she is still my sister. I could never deny that fact and not respond with an answer that includes her. If the person who is asking then inquires as to where Suzette lives, I tell them she lives in heaven.

*

MICHAEL SMITH
Michael's 39-year-old brother Patrick
was killed by an impaired driver in 2007

I have one sibling: Patrick.

*

DAWN WOINOVICK
Dawn's 52-year-old brother
Todd died from cancer in 2013

In our family, my brother Todd and I were the only children. And because of there being only two of us, we had either a very tight and close relationship or a very competitive one. However, our personalities were very different so that made for some interesting times. Todd was always the quiet and sneaky one, so even though he was older I protected him from bullies because I was very tomboyish, outgoing and angry.

CHAPTER SIX

THE DATES

There are certain sorrows that never fade away until
the heart stops beating and the last breath is taken.
-UNKNOWN

Our expectations and memories of balloons and cakes and presents
are as regular as the rising sun. When our sibling passes, however,
how do we celebrate the life that is no more? And how do we
acknowledge the painful date that marks their death?

*

EMILY BAIRD-LEVINE
Emily's 43-year-old brother Don
died from a heart attack in 2004

There really hasn't been a set ritual. On Don's birthday my
husband and kids sometimes do something fun that Don would
have liked to do. One year when my niece was visiting, we did a
rope course nearby. That is something Don would enjoy. Other
times, we eat something yummy that Don liked. Keeping it light
and fun seems to be the theme of the birthday.

The anniversary of Don's death has changed and varied over
the years. Most years, I make a donation in Don's memory to his
alma mater, Pomona College. It is for forty-seven dollars because

for some reason unbeknown to me, there is a significance of the number forty-seven at Pomona. I carry on that tradition. A few years after Don died, I decided to observe the anniversary of his death within the Jewish tradition. This day is called a *yahrzeit*. You need a minion to have a yahrzeit service at the synagogue. The mourning's prayer is read in Hebrew by the family member or by someone else at the service who no longer has living parents. The service is about celebrating life. It is followed by a blessing over wine or grape juice and a meal or snacks. The food is spicy, yummy food that Don liked. I do like getting together with other people in a prescribed manner. It makes it more clear what is to happen. This past year we celebrated the lives of two other people who had lost loved ones at around the same time of year, in years past. We were all at different stages of loss. We shared about our loved ones.

Sometimes as the years go by, it gets more sad to me. I feel like Don is farther and farther away from me. I wish I had more memories to experience. This is definitely a painful time.

*

CHRISTINE BASTONE
Christine's 38-year-old sister
Liz died by suicide in 2012

For my sister's birthday, I bake some frosted brownies as a kind of cake, invite my parents over, light one candle and put it on the cake, put said cake in the middle of my kitchen table, have my son record us singing "Happy Birthday," and upload the video to YouTube. Well the uploading part doesn't come until later. And of course we do all eat a piece of her cake.

I also donate a book to my local library that's dedicated to Liz as a sort of gift to my sister. This is always something on the subject of suicide, or is somehow related to the subject of suicide. For Liz's first birthday after she died, I also cooked a dinner that she would have liked. I also hosted a Facebook event for her. That was a bit much to do again though. So now I just do the cake and the gift.

The one thing that I didn't expect was how difficult my birthday was. That definitely took me by surprise! I expected Liz's birthday to be difficult. But that wasn't too bad. Maybe because I am still able to do things to observe the day, and honor her. But on my birthday, the thing that I want the most is a card from my baby sister. And unfortunately that is the one thing that I cannot have.

For my sister's death anniversary, I host a Facebook event. I've made it to be like an online memorial service. There are pictures of flowers, there are YouTube videos, there is something that I've written for the occasion such as an updated eulogy. There is a slideshow. There are a few videos of me playing hand bell solos. There are pictures with pretty online frames, and there are collages. I work on it little by little all year. A lot of times I work on it on the tenth of the month, those are the "monthaversary" days. And it not only keeps me busy, but gives me something very important to do on those anniversary days that I'm sure would be much more difficult to deal with if I didn't do something like that.

*

SHANNON BOOS
Shannon's 21-year-old brother Kevin
was killed by two drunk drivers in 2015

We lost Kevin just over a year ago, and have only celebrated one of his birthdays and one death anniversary so far.

Kevin was born on December 6, 1993, and was killed exactly three months before his twenty-second birthday.

We were dreading his birthday. It was so scary and horrible to think that it was his twenty-second birthday, but he wasn't really turning twenty-two. He is forever twenty-one. However, we decided that the best way to get through it was to celebrate, and to remember him in some form or another.

Family and friends gathered at his gravesite wearing sports shirts or jerseys of his favorite teams (Miami Dolphins, Miami Heat, Miami Marlins, Florida Panthers, etc.). When everyone gathered, I gave a short speech about how grateful we were to see their faces there, and then gave people time to meditate, talk, etc. We then gathered at a family friend's house and had a celebration for Kevin. Although it did help a lot to see family and friends and to talk about him in positive ways, I do remember feeling pain, of course. Pain that he wasn't there. Pain that he should be there. Pain that I was not with him. Pain. Pain. Pain.

The one-year anniversary was very hard, harder than I had actually anticipated. Now that it has passed, I still find myself thinking, what was Kevin doing this time last year? And then I remember that he was dead and buried seven feet underground, and I feel a kick in the gut.

Something I am grateful for throughout this whole experience is my newfound relationship and friendship with Hayley Carr, Morgan's sister. Because we both lost our siblings in the same crash, we have a bond and understanding of each other that we cannot find with many others. Hayley and I got together and planned a memorial for the one-year anniversary. We spent a good couple of months planning, brainstorming, advertising the event, and making it happen. We wanted it to be perfect, because we believe that our three angels deserve no less. We created an event on Facebook called "Remembering Our Three Angels" and invited anyone and everyone. We made it clear that even if someone didn't know any of our three angels, they were welcome and encouraged to come. About three hundred and fifty people came. It was incredible. We had everyone wear clothing or colors that symbolized either Kevin, Morgan, or Vincenzo. So everyone was wearing jerseys, sports T-shirts, or anything else that reminded them of one or all of the three.

We created personalized boxes for each of them. I made Kevin's box Miami Dolphins-themed, his favorite team. We had people write letters, thoughts, or memories on index cards and put them in the box. We also had members of each family speak about whatever their heart desired. We then passed out candles and held a moment of silence at 9:15 p.m., the time of the crash. I was honestly dreading the ceremony when it finally came time to get ready. I wanted to crawl into bed and disappear; I just wanted the day to end. However, I knew I needed to do it because Kevin, Vincenzo, and Morgan were counting on me. I am so glad I pushed through, because the ceremony was so incredible, and so beautiful, and went so perfectly. I knew they were there; of course they were, because they made it so obvious. When we arrived at the park, the weather was rather gross. The skies were gray and cloudy, and the air was very humid and sticky. About thirty minutes before the event started, the sky opened up into a beautiful array of colors so magnificent that a picture could not do it justice.

If I learned one thing through this process of reaching anniversaries, it is that we need to do something. We need to have some sort of event, whether big or small, to remember them. To celebrate them. To gather and talk and reminisce and cry. Because no matter how hard we try to push it away and forget, it will still be there. It will always be there.

*

LISA FORESTBIRD
Lisa's 40-year-old brother Rob died
from a pontine hemorrhage in 2006

This year I forced myself to have a party on the anniversary of my brother's death. I had to schedule the party, so I decided to do so on Rob's anniversary. I thought it would be nice to be with others, but it took a lot of energy. A lot of energy to pull it together and then to keep a happy face. It seems every year I reinvent the wheel — I do much better when I just give myself space to be mellow and alone and introspective. Every year I somehow think I should be living life more outwardly, but that isn't always the best thing.

I have found every year around the anniversary of Rob's death, if I don't create some intentional space, life creates it for me. To me intentional space means I carry out life's duties like going to work, but I don't bring any more activity into my life than I need to.

My mom happened to be in town for Rob's birthday. I savored the time I had with my mom but it was bittersweet all day. Several things happened that day, three to be exact, and all of them were good. I attributed each to be a gift from Rob.

Rob was in a coma for six days, starting September 12. Labor Day is generally when my melancholy starts and intensifies closer to his death. I find it is absolutely necessary for me to have that down time from around September 12 to September 17. But really, there is no getting around it — each anniversary is really painful.

*

BONNIE FORSHEY
Bonnie's 54-year-old sister Eunice
died from bladder cancer in 2010

In addition to my sister, Eunice, I have two deceased brothers. I write a small article on their birthdates, anniversary dates, and holidays. I also place flowers on their graves.

*

LAURA HABEDANK
Laura's brother Brian died
by suicide in 2010 at age 35

It's been so important to me to not let these days go by unacknowledged. I have a variety of things I do that help me get through these days. I do any and all of the following: order pizza and watch Brian's favorite movie, look through pictures of him, watch the photographic memorial my dad put together, light a candle for Brian, listen to some of his favorite music, take a walk to the tree where I've spread some of his ashes or write a letter to him.

I have some wonderful friends who have joined me on some of these occasions and are gracious enough to listen to me share stories about Brian and my favorite memories of him, and offer a shoulder and a box of Kleenex for the times when it's all too much to handle. Those days I definitely experience the loss more profoundly, because it's painful to be celebrating these days without him. But I know I'd feel much worse if I didn't take the time to remember Brian in a way that's special to me and would have been special to him.

*

MARCELLA MALONE
Marcella's 20-year-old brother
Michael died by suicide in 2014

Michael's death being only a year and a half ago, my family hasn't really established any traditions for these days. The wound is simply too deep for that. On what would have been his twenty-first birthday, just six months after his passing, we hosted a memorial lantern launch from the high school's old football field, where he did much of his playing and made many great memories. It was nice to be surrounded that day by all the friends and family who loved him. The event was beautiful, despite the wind making it almost impossible to get a lantern in the air. I know Michael got some smiles out of our struggles.

Since then we have not had any special events, nor do we get together. Instead, we have made it a goal within our family and a plea to our Facebook community to complete acts of kindness toward others on these days in Michael's memory. You never know the struggles going on in someone's life. Even something as simple as a smile could improve someone's day or even save his or her life. As I perform these acts, I make sure to leave a note with an encouraging message and some words about that day's significance to me and the amazing person my brother was.

These days also make me remember the importance of family, and I take the time on each of them to make sure they all know how much they are loved, whether it be in person or via the phone. Much of my family does the same. It's truly the little things that make these days pass a little easier.

*

BROOKE NINNI MATTHEWS
Brooke's 31-year-old brother Timothy
died by homicide in 2012

Every birthday or "angelversary," as I like to call it, I try to acknowledge it somehow. On my brother's birthday I either let balloons go, or have a birthday cake, or something as simple as just cracking open a Rolling Rock beer. This past birthday, my son graduated and I held a graduation party for my son on my brother's birthday. My friend made brownies and we wrote, "Happy birthday, Timmy" on them for my brother. Many family and friends came to celebrate my son's graduation as well as to sing and celebrate my brother's birthday.

The first two years of his angelversary we held a benefit in honor of him, and the money we collected went to a nonprofit organization for homicide victims and their families left behind. On the third angelversary my daughter and I let green star balloons go; green was my brother's favorite color.

I do little extra things to acknowledge his birthday and angelversary, but I acknowledge and celebrate him every day. He was a tree trimmer and loved trees and nature, so to honor him I decorated some rooms in my home with tree and nature themes.

*

NICKI NOBLE
Nicki's 43-year-old brother Don
died from a heart attack in 2004

I sometimes post something on Facebook, call or message my siblings, and talk about my brother to my husband, kids and close friends. It makes me feel better although sad at the same time.

*

BRIDGET PARK
Bridget's brother Austin died
by suicide in 2008 at age 14

My family and I try to do something my brother liked to do, or eat his favorite food on his birthday, anniversary, etc. However, the anniversary is very difficult to acknowledge, because it is during Thanksgiving, usually one to three days after the holiday. We try to be around family and keep spirits high, because it is really easy to slip into a dark mindset.

My brother's birthday is the hardest for me to celebrate. Every year that goes by and in which he would have grown older, it makes me sad that we are not growing and experiencing life together. I am now twenty years old, and he would be twenty-two if he were still alive. What pains me the most is not having him there with me and not having a life together. I think about how it would have been to send him off to college or see him fall in love and get married. It is all the missed memories and milestones that hurt the most to me. His birthday is also very hard because he and my dad share the same birthday. My dad feels very guilty and sad on this day, because it is just not the same without my brother.

The key for getting through these hard holidays is having loved ones around me and keeping my brother's memory alive. I focus on the beautiful life he lived and not the tragic death he suffered. I think about the memories we were fortunate enough to have together, and I make sure to count them as blessings.

*

MICHAEL SMITH
Michael's 39-year-old brother Patrick
was killed by an impaired driver in 2007

It depends on where I am. Now that I live in Connecticut again, I visit his grave and tell him what's going on.

It still is difficult to relive the whole story, and it is upsetting that he is missing holidays, birthdays, seeing his son Dakota growing up and going to college, but we all remember Patrick in our own way.

*

DAWN WOINOVICK
Dawn's 52-year-old brother
Todd died from cancer in 2013

On Todd's death anniversary, my parents and I take balloons, write thoughts and prayers on them, and take flowers to the grave. We put a memorial in the newspaper and we read that, let the balloons go, and then go to my folks where Todd passed away and drink wine, talk about him, and basically just remember him more than usual. This year I watched my balloons go through the clouds I swear right to the gates of heaven.

For Todd's birthday, we go to dinner and celebrate like normal just without gifts. Both times are very emotional and the heart still misses him dearly. But the spirit knows he is free in heaven.

*

Tears don't
stop with years.

EMILY BAIRD-LEVINE

*

CHAPTER SEVEN

THE HOLIDAYS

The only predictable thing about grief is that it's unpredictable. -LYNDA CHELDELIN FELL

The holiday season comes around like clockwork, and for those in mourning, this time of year brings a kaleidoscope of emotions. If the grief is still fresh, the holidays can be downright raw. How do we navigate the invitations, decorations, and festivities that summon memories from yesteryear?

*

EMILY BAIRD-LEVINE
Emily's 43-year-old brother Don
died from a heart attack in 2004

We haven't lived very close to any family members in so long, so we hadn't been getting together for holidays with any of them, even before Don died. So, really holidays are about the same. The last time I talked to Don was a few weeks before he died, on my birthday. He and Kitty, his fiancée (we found out they were planning to get married from Kitty, after Don passed away), called me on my birthday. They sang to me and we chatted for a while. Don sounded great and like himself. My birthday has been very difficult ever since. I, for many years, didn't want to celebrate and didn't want to be wished a happy birthday. I had a groups of friends that used to go out to lunch for our birthdays. We continued to do so for all of them, but it became clear that I didn't want to go out for mine, especially on my actual birthday. They stopped wishing me a happy birthday. My family has been quite patient with me. They ask me every year what I want to do. I have started to plan my own birthday celebrations so not to inflict mixed feelings and indecision onto them. This is working out pretty well.

*

CHRISTINE BASTONE
Christine's 38-year-old sister
Liz died by suicide in 2012

That first year things were a bit different. But otherwise I pass the holiday season pretty close to how I used to do so before my sister died. Now I do have one of those pictures with the pretty online frames for all the different holidays. They are printed. And I like to touch them sometimes. This helps make me feel connected to my sister on the holidays. I also have a three-by-five picture of Liz in a frame, along with a few fake roses that are at my parents' house, which is where I spend most of my holidays. This is so in a way, it is like Liz is still here.

That first year, on all the holidays, all I felt was her absence. So the picture and the flowers were a successful attempt to not feel her absence quite so much. That first Christmas was absolutely excruciating. My biggest problem with Christmas was that it's a season, and not just a day. By that time I had learned to deal with a day...but I was dreadfully unprepared for the season of Christmas, which lasts about a month. The main reason that I was so unprepared for Christmas was that I simply ran out of time. I spent so much time that first year figuring out how to handle all the other holidays, especially Thanksgiving, that unfortunately there was no time left to prepare for Christmas. These days it might be Thanksgiving that is the worst. My sister's Thanksgiving vacation to Florida in 2011 was the last time I saw her alive. Thanksgiving itself is usually okay, it's the whole weekend after Thanksgiving that is so very, very painful. The past three and a half years holidays have definitely gotten easier. But that doesn't mean that they are easy, or that they will be easy any time soon.

*

SHANNON BOOS
Shannon's 21-year-old brother Kevin
was killed by two drunk drivers in 2015

Only one holiday season has passed since Kevin was killed, and it actually came pretty quickly after he died, as he was killed in September.

Thanksgiving was the worst. I remember always loving Thanksgiving, as most people do, because it is all about food, family, and more food.

Kevin also loved Thanksgiving. His favorite part was always the mashed potatoes and the corn. He was a starch kind of guy.

I remember one year in particular, circa 2008, when we were playing football with our family while dinner was cooking. Kevin and I were on opposite teams and were both running to catch the ball. He did manage to catch the ball, but banged the bottom of his chin fairly hard on the top of my head in the process.

Anyone who knew Kevin knew that when he was focusing and concentrating really hard, he stuck his tongue out. Not just the tip of his tongue; his entire tongue would hang out of his mouth anytime he had to put a lot of thinking into something. Well, for Kevin, catching a football required his ridiculous "tongue face," so while he banged his chin on my head, his teeth managed to go through his tongue.

Needless to say, it was difficult for him to eat his Thanksgiving dinner that year.

Thanksgiving is the first holiday I think about when I think about Kevin. It was his favorite. And now that he isn't here, I am not sure how we are going to keep "celebrating" without him.

This first Thanksgiving was weird. I'm sure that people outside of this horrible "sibling loss club" will think of the word "weird" as an inappropriate description of something like this, but I know that all of you who are in this awful club know exactly what I mean.

The empty chair, the empty plate. The fact that there were still plenty of mashed potatoes for everyone to eat. The lack of laughter and smiles. The presence of tears, frowns, silence, and heartbreak. It was all so weird. And so gut-wrenching.

I remember waking up Thanksgiving morning and not really receiving text messages from friends. I'm still not sure if it was selfish of me to expect text messages of comfort from my friends, but I did. Not only was it my first Thanksgiving without Kevin, it was my first ever holiday without him.

I finally reached out myself. I texted a good friend of mine, explaining how much I was dreading the day, how much I wanted to avoid it, and how I wasn't sure if my heart was just shattered in pieces or completely withered away into nothing.

Her response? "Shannon you need to stop being so negative and think about what you *are* thankful for."

What I am thankful for? How the f*** am I supposed to be grateful on a day like today? I can't even really think about that response without feeling my blood boil.

We did carry on through the day, however. I remember that my dad, who lives in another state from my family and me, could not make it for Thanksgiving, and it made it so much weirder and so much emptier.

A family who usually celebrated Thanksgiving the traditional American way now sat around a table at an unfamiliar restaurant, desperately filling the deafening silence with comments about food that I can't even remember the taste of.

Christmas was just as weird, and just as awful. Before Kevin died, I was the typical person who looked forward to Christmas every year, blasting "All I Want for Christmas Is You," and buying gifts for loved ones.

This year was no doubt different. Because now I turned off the radio anytime my favorite Christmas song came on, because now all I wanted for Christmas was Kevin.

I hate the holidays. And I truly feel that I always will. The dreaded time of year is rapidly approaching, and I can't get time to slow down no matter how hard I try. They will never, ever be the same without my Kevin and his mashed potatoes.

*

LISA FORESTBIRD
Lisa's 40-year-old brother Rob died
from a pontine hemorrhage in 2006

It was profusely hard to start with but I've learned to adjust. The first holiday season, I felt like an orphan and tried to create new memories with existing family members. I just kind of resigned myself to the fact that Rob would no longer be one of the people with whom I would celebrate the holidays.

The first few years, I put a white candle at our dinner table and I had myself convinced the candle was Rob. I would cry when I looked at the candle. The second holiday season was even harder because my little brother had decided to spend Christmas with his new girlfriend, who by the next Christmas had become his wife. While I was delighted to have Angie join our family, it also felt like I had lost Jim as well.

In the ensuing years, I have come to accept the changes. I have gotten to know Angie's family and it is a new tradition that we spend some time at the holiday with her family. I try to create my own traditions too, and convince myself life can still be rich even when it is different. I guess Rob's death anniversary is the hardest. Christmas was very hard but I've found ways to temper that. I guess Rob's birthday is the happiest of holidays.

*

BONNIE FORSHEY
Bonnie's 54-year-old sister Eunice
died from bladder cancer in 2010

My holidays are no longer happy. I just sleep through them; nothing to celebrate or be happy about. I have no one to cook for or buy presents for. I merely exist now.

*

LAURA HABEDANK
Laura's brother Brian died
by suicide in 2010 at age 35

The only holidays that really sting are Thanksgiving and Christmas, as those were the ones that were the most important to

Brian and to our whole family. Brian absolutely adored Thanksgiving, because he loved food and he loved football, both of which he could get a whole bunch of on that day. There was something so soothing about being with family, playing games and laughing, enjoying a large, lovely meal and then falling asleep on the couch to the soothing sound of a football game on the TV.

Christmas is extra hard on me because I have so many fond memories of that time of year. I so adored shopping for presents for Brian; we knew each other so well and always had fun picking out great things for each other and thoroughly enjoyed watching each other open the gifts we exchanged. It often involved at least one gag gift that left us crying tears of laughter. And Brian had just about the best laugh of anyone in the world. It was so incredibly contagious, and I loved being able to bring that out in him so much.

With Brian gone, and all my grandparents gone, I have so little family left that I've pretty much lost most of my interest in the holidays, because the people who made them so special aren't here anymore. I don't get as much enjoyment out of the foods, sounds, sights, and traditions that go along with that time of year anymore. I guess because it's all a reminder of the things I've lost along the way. I have great friends who have welcomed me as part of their family celebrations and I appreciate it so very much... but it's hard not to feel out of place there. I find myself looking around the table, at the siblings joking with one another and just ache with jealousy because I so badly want what they have and I can't have it.

For Christmas and for Brian's birthday I've made it a new tradition to either buy gifts for those less fortunate or donate money to suicide awareness organizations in his memory, because it feels good to give to others when I'm hurting — to turn the pain into something good for someone else.

*

MARCELLA MALONE
Marcella's 20-year-old brother
Michael died by suicide in 2014

Since the loss of Michael, holidays are much harder for my family. There is an obvious void. However, we choose not to let this missing piece take these celebrations away from us. We celebrate for us, for him, and in memory of everyone we have lost. If anything, Michael's loss has made these celebrations more important. Everyone goes to my parents' for each holiday, and we do our best to reflect on the good times and enjoy ourselves while providing the support we need from one another to get through the day. For me the biggest difference is the sadness that hits on the morning of each holiday. That's when it hits me that Michael won't be there, and it almost always results in a complete breakdown on my part. Once it's over, the importance of all the family I have left kicks in, and I do my best to see as many of them as possible, and make sure my boyfriend gets to do the same, celebrating more powerfully than ever before, for now I truly know to never take these moments for granted.

*

BROOKE NINNI MATTHEWS
Brooke's 31-year-old brother Timothy
died by homicide in 2012

Holidays are a lot different since my brother's death, I wouldn't say they are any harder than his birthday and angelversary. I find every day is hard without him, some days are harder than others; it depends on the day of the grief rollercoaster.

The family would get together on the big holidays like Thanksgiving, Easter, Christmas Eve, and Christmas. Since my brother's death, my siblings and I just kind of do our own things with our husbands, kids, or friends. We all seem to have gone our separate ways, and don't have that closeness like we used to. It was as though my brother was the glue that held the siblings together. We still occasionally get together for little events and some holidays.

*

NICKI NOBLE
Nicki's 43-year-old brother Don
died from a heart attack in 2004

Due to the fact that my brother died on December 26, the holidays are bittersweet. I try to reflect on the positive memories at that time. That doesn't always happen. It has been eleven years this coming holiday season and it is still painful. I got the call on December 24 that Don had had a heart attack, and my husband rushed to the hospital late that night. It is at times such a horrible blur. It still gives me shivers when I think about those few days.

*

MICHAEL SMITH
Michael's 39-year-old brother Patrick
was killed by an impaired driver in 2007

Holidays, I have to say, don't have the same meaning for me now. After my brother's death my parents began to age more rapidly. My father's hair went white and my mother became quiet. I moved home so they would not be alone. My brother lived locally in Connecticut, while I had lived on the West Coast and elsewhere for many years. I haven't had a Christmas tree since Pat was killed, and I don't think my parents have either. Since he was divorced, his son Dakota spent time with Pat on preplanned dates and there was a poor communication with his ex-wife. After his death, Dakota's family moved to South Carolina, and he has little to no communication with his grandparents. In short, holidays are just long quiet days.

*

DAWN WOINOVICK
Dawn's 52-year-old brother
Todd died from cancer in 2013

Wow, holidays. Okay, well, we still don't really celebrate but that's not all because of Todd, or I'm in denial which is also partly true. All my kids are grown and only one celebrates holidays, so I celebrate with her, but I'm trying to start a new normal this year. It has only been year two since my brother passed. Year one it just felt like no celebration, I didn't feel like it. But the new normal has happened for me to move on.

All holidays without your loved one are difficult but in order to grow through the grief process and respect my brother's life, I need to live mine so when I meet him in heaven I will be able to say I loved him this much.

*

CHAPTER EIGHT

THE BELONGINGS

Siblings are merely different flowers that all grew
from the same garden. -LYNDA CHELDELIN FELL

Our brother's and sister's belongings are a direct connection to
what once was. They are what is left of our childhood memories.
When does the time come to address the painful task of sorting
through the memory-laden belongings? Who handles such a task?

*

EMILY BAIRD-LEVINE
Emily's 43-year-old brother Don
died from a heart attack in 2004

Don's belongings were handled by Kitty, his fiancée. They had
been living together in his apartment along with Don's dog, El Nina
Junior. Kitty went through Don's belongings, as she could while
going through her own grieving process. She stayed in the
apartment with Junior. At one point, when I was visiting with my
sister Nicki in San Diego, Kitty came to see us and brought us some
boxes of pictures and papers that Don had ended up with after our
parents passed away several years prior. There weren't any issues
distributing anything. The only emotions that came up through this

process was the loss of Don and the necessity for sorting and distributing things from his apartment. It seemed that there was some healing that took place between Nicki, Kitty, and I while looking through the boxes of things.

A few sort of funny things happened while Kitty was cleaning out Don's apartment. After my mom, of blessed memory, passed away in 1997, Don ended up with her ashes that we had planned on distributing somewhere. We just hadn't yet figured out the most appropriate location. Well, in a very Don-like way and to keep the ashes in a secure place, Don "hid" them, so to speak. And he hid them so well that Kitty had quite the time trying to locate them among all of the many interesting things that Don had accumulated over the years. Unlike some people who prominently display an urn on their mantel, Don had put the box of ashes from the crematorium in the back of a closet, behind many other things like perhaps linen. Kitty, after much searching, located them. That was a relief.

Before Kitty came down to see my sister and me in San Diego, she called and asked if we wanted some of the succulent plants that Don had acquired, from the house we grew up in, after my mom died. My sister and I were so emphatic about not wanting these particular plants. Kitty hadn't heard, I presume, the story of how these plants got to our family home to begin with and really thought we would have wanted them. When we were kids, our great-aunt Tilly would show up at our house, mostly unannounced I believe, with cactus and succulent plants to plop wherever there was room in our yard. Tilly wasn't our favorite great-aunt or my mom's favorite aunt. I never liked those plants and certainly didn't need to have even one of them! Don had a green thumb and apparently liked those plants enough to take them and replant them. I chuckle now at this whole thing.

*

CHRISTINE BASTONE
Christine's 38-year-old sister
Liz died by suicide in 2012

I didn't handle any of Liz's belongings. I'm sure that it was her husband who did that. I just wish that I would have thought to ask shortly after it happened if I could have just a few of her things. Because I would dearly love to have a few of them.

*

SHANNON BOOS
Shannon's 21-year-old brother Kevin
was killed by two drunk drivers in 2015

My brother and I always looked incredibly similar from the time we were infants, all the way up until he died while we were in college. We both were also very small, which I am now grateful for. I say this because I claimed almost every one of his T-shirts, besides the ones anyone else in my family wanted. I wear them all the time, sometimes just around the house, sometimes to bed, but mostly when I am missing him and want to feel him close to me.

My brother, my parents, and I all found a way to split up Kevin's belongings. His things are all with one of us somewhere in the family, whether it is with one of the four of us or with our grandmother or our cousins. That is something I am grateful for. I know how important it is to me to have some of his things with me, so I made sure to give something of his to anyone who wanted it.

I have quite a few of his shirts and jackets, and I wear them all the time. I also have a stuffed animal that he had when he was a baby, a dog that he named Applesauce. It sits on my dresser and leaves happy thoughts of him in my head when I see it.

There are two of Kevin's belongings that are the most important to me. One of them was actually a gift of a family friend. A few days after Kevin was killed, this friend asked for a bag of Kevin's T-shirts or any other clothing, as she wanted to make us something out of it. On the one-year anniversary, she finally finished her amazing gift. She sewed together four quilts, one for my brother Jeffrey, one for each of my parents, and one for me. All four quilts are made entirely of his clothing, from his pajama pants, sports jerseys, and T-shirts. I sleep with it at night, and will hold it right up to my nose, hoping that his scent will bring him to my dreams.

The belonging that tops all of these others isn't really a belonging of his; it was a part of him. The funeral home that helped us with Kevin's burial was nice enough to cut off locks of Kevin's hair before he was buried. A few months later my father purchased necklaces for each member of our family, and inside each one is a lock of his hair. I wear it all the time, every day. No object has ever been so important to me, and I am so grateful to have him so close to my heart, especially on the days I need it the most.

*

LISA FORESTBIRD
Lisa's 40-year-old brother Rob died
from a pontine hemorrhage in 2006

My parents handled my brother's belongings, and I think that was probably a useful thing for them to do as part of the grieving process. When my brother passed away, I was living in Detroit and he in Illinois. Since my parents made me focus on my job, they pretty much handled Rob's possessions all by themselves. We have worked hard to find loving homes for many of his possessions. His remaining things, nine years later, are still in a storage locker.

I have many of Rob's things and they have brought me great comfort, especially since I moved two thousand miles away just before the one-year anniversary of his death. They are a constant reminder of Rob and help remind me I need to build new and good memories with things such as his kitchen table, dishes, silverware, and desk. I also have a guest room set up much as he did with the same furniture and furnishings — that too is a nice reminder of where Rob left off.

*

BONNIE FORSHEY
Bonnie's 54-year-old sister Eunice
died from bladder cancer in 2010

When my sister died, she left behind three children. My niece was in her thirties and I helped her to go through my sister's house. We donated a lot of things and had a sale to get rid of the rest. It was very hard to go through the things that my sister had treasured. The children picked out everything that they wanted and we got rid of everything else. The house had to be sold and the money was shared between the three of them. My sister had turned into a hoarder and it was quite an ordeal going through everything. We had to clean the entire house, scrape off wallpaper, paint, and have remodeling done. It was difficult to see all traces of my sister vanish. I spent my life with her, and now she is gone. I can't even drive by her home now without becoming emotional.

*

LAURA HABEDANK
Laura's brother Brian died
by suicide in 2010 at age 35

Just three days after getting the phone call telling me my only brother had taken his own life, I found myself in his condo with my family cleaning out all his belongings. It felt so wrong being there going through everything he owned; it felt like a betrayal of his privacy in a way. I still hadn't fully grasped that it was real and I fully expected to see him come walking through the door and ask us to knock it off.

It turns out that in his final few months Brian had fallen behind in his mortgage payments because he'd been out of full-time work for a year. That was so unlike him, because he was undoubtedly the most responsible person I had ever known. The last we spoke about it, he had been months ahead in his payments, had money in savings, and was doing just fine. But the more depressed he grew, the less drive he had to go out and pursue a job when, in his mind, he wouldn't be around for much longer.

The real estate market had taken such a terrible turn and the housing values in his neighborhood had dramatically plummeted, and the balance of the loan was far greater than the home's value. So there we were hastily trying to empty his home of everything he owned as quickly as possible. Some went into the dumpster, some we donated to a neighbor of Brian's who was in need of some furnishings, but the majority of it went into our vehicles and trailer. We planned to get as much as we could in one trip, and walk away from it. It was all very rushed. I can't adequately explain everything I was feeling that day, but I did feel a bit of shame. We walked away knowing full well that the bank would soon be coming to foreclose on the house. I was embarrassed for Brian, because as responsible as he was, I know he wouldn't have wanted to be remembered for skirting any responsibility, financial or otherwise.

I didn't pay much attention to Brian's things until they were all I had left of him. But after he died, I found myself irrationally attached to anything that belonged to him, anything he had touched. I immediately regretted that we had thrown away anything at all. I suddenly wanted to keep every single pen with which he ever wrote, every sample of his handwriting, every shirt he had ever worn, and every glass from which he had sipped too much vodka in the days leading up to his death. They were all precious to me; if he had touched it, I wanted to save it.

We sold his car a few weeks later, and that too felt wrong. I was still holding out hope that it was all somehow just a terrible misunderstanding and he'd show up any day looking for all his stuff. I kept his big TV, and I treasure it so much. I'm sure it sounds silly, but the TV was on when he was found. I know it was one of the last things he looked at; it was in the room with him when he died. I have his laptop, and never imagined that someday I'd be typing these horrifying words on it.

There are a few things of Brian's that hold extra special meaning for me, the things that were extra special to him. I often wear his Jack Del Rio jersey, his favorite flannel pajama pants, and his favorite hooded sweatshirt. I sleep every night with the blanket I crocheted as a gift for his very last birthday; it was purple and gold for the Minnesota Vikings and he was so proud of it.

The police report said Brian had the blanket on his lap when he died. I like to imagine that he felt some comfort having that blanket with him and that he felt as much love for him coming out of that blanket as I put into every single stitch of it.

As much as I value all these things, I'd give anything to be able to trade them all back for just one more day with him.

*

MARCELLA MALONE
Marcella's 20-year-old brother
Michael died by suicide in 2014

Within the first couple of weeks after Michael's death, the immediate family chose the items they wanted for comfort or remembering him. Other than that, Michael's room and belongings remained sat they were for a couple of months. Entering it was too painful for any of us. About three months later, my cousin came and spent the weekend with my mom to help her start going through Michael's room. They accomplished quite a bit, but mostly just organizing and getting rid of garbage; his room was never very clean. Having neutral support was very helpful and necessary for my mom throughout that task.

Since then, very little has been done. Occasionally someone will go in and look around, but that's about it. Once the one year anniversary had passed, our family began to use his things we needed. I have some of his electronics, and my older brother has Michael's hunting gear. We decided it was better to use it and honor him than let it sit. My parents also gave some of Michael's belongings, like his weight equipment, to his close friends who could use it. It will be a long time before his room is altered to become something other than his room. Eighteen months just isn't enough to make it seem real that Michael really isn't coming home.

For Christmas this year I am working on a project for my son and nephew with some of Michael's old clothes. Although he never got to meet them, he was excited to be an uncle and I know he's with them. I want to make sure they know him.

*

BROOKE NINNI MATTHEWS
Brooke's 31-year-old brother Timothy
died by homicide in 2012

My sisters and I divided my brother's belongings between us. I made a memory quilt with his clothes for myself, my daughter and my sisters. I also added photos of us together on the quilt.

*

NICKI NOBLE
Nicki's 43-year-old brother Don
died from a heart attack in 2004

My sweet brother was engaged to a beautiful and kind lady. She handled his things overall. My siblings and I gathered and distributed some family photos, etc. There were no issues between the siblings. Looking at and remembering our childhood while looking through the photos was very hard and sad but healing at the same time. My sweet brother had a great sense of humor, so many photos reflected his funny personality. I still tear up when I look at his photos but smile at the same time.

*

BRIDGET PARK
Bridget's brother Austin died
by suicide in 2008 at age 14

My family and I waited a long time to box up my brother's belongings, around six to eight months. We left his room untouched, exactly how he left it, so we could go in there and feel like he was still living in it. I know that my mom would go and sit on Austin's bed and talk to him like she used to when he was alive. It was nice to see all of his stuff and not look deeper than surface level at his belongings and his life. Soon we realized that we needed to move on, and learn how to keep his memory alive in other ways.

*

MARYELLEN ROACH
MaryEllen's 41-year-old sister Suzette
died in a car accident in 2012

A couple of days after the funeral my parents, younger sister Ashley, her husband Moi, and I all began going through their things at my parent's house where Suzette and the girls had lived for five years. It felt like an invasion of their privacy, especially Suzette's, and it was hard to make my mind accept that she would not be back to wear her clothes or makeup, listen to her CDs, watch her DVDs, read her books, cross-stitch anything else, or use any of her other things. It was difficult for me to claim things of hers that I wanted to keep, because it made me feel like a vulture picking over what she left behind.

Our mom, Ashley, and I kept a lot of Suzette's clothes to wear and donated the things we couldn't or wouldn't wear. My mom kept most of her jewelry, but gave both Ashley and me pieces we would wear. I kept a lot of Suzette's makeup to both wear and also keep just because it was hers. Ashley and I divided Suzette's books and her DVDs according to what we liked. Suzette loved to cross-stitch and had lots of thread, patterns, and other supplies. Since none of us cross-stitch, I gave all of those things to my friend Christina who felt honored to have them. I kept all of Suzette's CDs and even cassette tapes whether I liked the music or not, because music was so important to Suzette and because they will always make me think of her.

I also had to go through Suzette's room at my house, which I requested to do alone. I found a ticket for the Celtic Thunder concert that was to take place on November 8, 2012. Suzette had found that she could get a great seat if she went by herself. The ticket for the upcoming concert was for the third row in the center of the St. Louis Fox Theater, a fantastic seat. I debated what to do with the ticket because I knew it would be an extremely emotional event if I used her ticket and attended the concert. I knew I would be overcome with the thought that I shouldn't be in that seat, but Suzette should be there as she intended. The concert would be November 8, which is the day after Lillian's birthday, the first one without her. The last time I had seen Celtic Thunder in concert was with Suzette and the girls at the same venue. I didn't know what to do, so I kept the ticket in a safe place while I contemplated and prayed about it. Finally, I felt peace about going and knew that Suzette would want me to use the ticket she bought with her hard-earned money and enjoy the concert. She had been really excited about going and had already laid out the outfit she would wear, down to the purse and shoes, which I still have. Mind you, she had done that in July and the concert wasn't until November.

When I attended the concert, I could feel Suzette next to me, so thankfully it wasn't quite as upsetting as I expected and I didn't feel guilty that I was in her seat. Most of the songs reminded me of Suzette and the girls, but none really upset me except for "A Place in the Choir," because that was a song played at their funeral.

It was incredibly difficult going through their belongings so early on, but I'm thankful we did because I found her ticket and was able to attend the concert with her. The original question was asking how I handled my sister's belongings, basically we tried to do what we thought Suzette would have wanted done with it all. We all kept things that remind us of her and we cherish the things we have. Sometimes it still feels strange because I have things that are hers, but they're mine now, but they're still hers. Although I know she's not coming back for her things, I still treat them all with the same respect and care as if she was.

*

MICHAEL SMITH
Michael's 39-year-old brother Patrick
was killed by an impaired driver in 2007

My parents boxed everything up and put it all into storage, where it stayed untouched for two years. During the summer when I was visiting from California I decided to open everything up and make decisions on what to do with his belongings and clothes. I gave some things to our friends and relatives, made donations, and kept some things.

It was difficult to do, because when Pat left for work that morning like any other day, his life was paused. It was difficult to see things he had worked so hard to afford cast into boxes and sitting idle. There are some of his clothes I kept for myself, and small items from around the house, but I gave many things to people who could use them and personal items to my parents, his son Dakota and other people.

*

DAWN WOINOVICK
Dawn's 52-year-old brother
Todd died from cancer in 2013

I handle Todd's belongings like treasures. His room at my folks' house is still the same. Going in there is peaceful. There is a tee shirt hanging on his bed post that still has his scent. I know this probably sounds strange, but it's true.

*

CHAPTER NINE

THE DARKNESS

Walking with a friend in the dark is better than walking alone in the light. -HELEN KELLER

Suicidal thoughts occur for some in the immediate aftermath of profound loss, yet few readily admit it for fear of being judged or condemned. While there would be no rainbow without the rain, where do we find the energy to fight the storm?

*

EMILY BAIRD-LEVINE
Emily's 43-year-old brother Don
died from a heart attack in 2004

I never had suicidal thoughts when Don died. I did experience some thoughts of why was it that Don was diagnosed with diabetes and not me. Why was Don the one handed the diabetes card, along with all of the complications that ensued from it? Perhaps I had some guilt for being one of the surviving siblings, but not to the point of wanting to take my own life.

*

CHRISTINE BASTONE
Christine's 38-year-old sister
Liz died by suicide in 2012

I have had suicidal thoughts since Liz died. Although that very first night after I learned that she had died, and I learned how it feels to lose a loved one this way, I decided that I would never so much as consider suicide ever again. But unfortunately life doesn't work that way. I would soon have such thoughts. They come on very suddenly. They also come on very strong, but thankfully they usually last only a few minutes. And the longest they last is a few hours. They were really scary at first. I would go to bed and just lie there, not moving, until the feeling went away. I felt that if I didn't let myself do anything, I couldn't hurt myself. Even though they were so short-lived, I still wanted to find a different way to deal with them. So I found two friends who, I could share with when I felt that way. A lot of times what I shared with them was just something I needed to say. It wasn't even necessarily what I believed, it was just the thoughts going around and around in my head. And getting them out of my head seemed to help.

I also read a few things that helped me. The first thing was that suicide happens when a person's pain exceeds his or her resources to handle that pain. And while that is simple, and being suicidal is complex, I do not find it simplistic. More than once I have taken a piece of paper, put a line down the middle of it, and written "Reduce Pain" on one side and "Increase Resources" on the other, and then listed ways that I could do both. Doing that exercise, even before any changes are actually made, has helped all by itself.

The second thing was that when you're suicidal, you have a need to change something for which you would rather die than go on living without. And to use suicidal feelings as a catalyst for that change, it makes the feelings empowering instead of so negative. I love this. And this is how I try to look at any suicidal feelings now. So, yes, I have had thoughts of suicide since Liz's death. But, thankfully, they have been just thoughts, and I have not been actively suicidal. And thankfully I have also found constructive ways to deal with them.

*

SHANNON BOOS
Shannon's 21-year-old brother Kevin
was killed by two drunk drivers in 2015

Before Kevin even died I was having mental issues. I was battling depression and anxiety. Kevin was one of the few people in my life who actually stood by me through it all. He was by my side through every up and down, and was one of the rare people who actually cared enough to check on me. Had I realized that I was going to lose him just a few months later, I would have thanked him a million times over.

After Kevin was killed I was swallowed into depression's hole deeper than I had ever been before. Getting out of bed was physically painful, and any sort of effort to get back into my normal routine was dreadful to think about. I wanted to die, I wanted to be with my brother more than anything. Wherever he was, I didn't care, I would go. I wanted to be there and protect him and hold him and he could do the same for me. I made the mistake of telling this to someone once, and the person threatened to call the police and have them take me to a hospital. Although I understood why they warned me, I was just trying to be honest. Why would I want to be in a world where my brother was gone?

There was one time I actually came close to committing suicide, although I do not remember it at all. I had been prescribed a medication by my psychiatrist to help with my anxiety and panic attacks. In reality, I would take one whenever the pain was too much. I wanted to be consumed by sleep so I could drown out the screams in my head and the roar of emptiness in my heart. I would typically take this medication in the afternoon as part of my new routine. I would wake up, lie in bed, take the medication, and sleep until about 7 p.m. Then I would get out of bed, drink a bottle of wine, and pass out again, drunk. It was a vicious cycle, but I didn't care. Nothing mattered anymore, and this was the closest thing I could feel to being dead without actually killing myself.

The only thing that kept me from actually killing myself was to spare my parents and my other brother the pain. I now knew firsthand what it was like to lose a sibling so traumatically, so I couldn't put my brother through that. I also saw the gut-wrenching pain that my parents were feeling every single day. The first time in my life that I ever saw my father cry was when we had to pick out a casket for Kevin, and I can still picture it over a year later. I could never willingly put my father or my mother, or anyone else for that matter, through something like that all over again.

One day the pain was substantially worse than usual. I could not sleep or eat. I couldn't even really breathe. I decided to take that magic pill a little earlier than normal. After thirty minutes of not feeling any relief, I decided to take a second one.

And then I blacked out.

The next thing I remember is waking up in a hospital, and answering questions about my mental history, all the while so exhausted that it was physically painful to speak.

Nine hours after I took that second pill, my roommates finally became aware that something was wrong when my dog, who was in the same room as me, was going crazy with panic. They found me unconscious and when I finally came to, I apparently kept saying over and over again, "I want to be with Kevin."

I had taken the rest of the bottle of those pills, along with a bottle of NyQuil and a bottle of wine. I later read my texts to my dad in which I kept saying that I was desperate for sleep. I remember nothing.

About a year has passed since this incident, and I am very grateful that this attempt was unsuccessful. The grief still consumes me at times, but I am very fortunate to have found a new love of life and the future. The pain of missing my brother is still so immense, but I know Kevin is happy to see me with a smile on my face, with eyes on the path in front of me.

*

LISA FORESTBIRD
Lisa's 40-year-old brother Rob died
from a pontine hemorrhage in 2006

No. On the contrary, I have had the urge to live a fuller life, to make up for lost time for Rob.

*

BONNIE FORSHEY
Bonnie's 54-year-old sister Eunice
died from bladder cancer in 2010

I became very depressed, but never thought of suicide. My sister left behind three children; I have to be here for them. They are all I have that ties me to her. I miss her so very much. The world was a better place when she was here.

*

LAURA HABEDANK
Laura's brother Brian died
by suicide in 2010 at age 35

Because of my own lifelong struggle with depression, I've thought about ending my own life more times than I could possibly count. But the level of despair and worthlessness I felt following Brian's death was immeasurable. I had lost all hope and couldn't possibly imagine myself having any quality of life at all if I even managed to survive. I couldn't shake the feeling of resenting him for taking his life when that was what I had wanted for myself so many times. Now that he had gone and done that, it would make me a real asshole to do that and leave Mom and Dad with no children at all. I hated the agony I was experiencing and wanted so badly to die. But there was nothing I could do about it; I felt as though he had stolen that option from me, and that upset me.

That being said, I've never been angry at him for his choice, because I've spent so much time in that place myself. I know how it feels to be experiencing a sadness of such depth and intensity and for such long periods of time that you aren't even capable of seeing any way through it at all. I know exactly what it's like to go to bed at night in such emotional agony that your body actually hurts and you pray so hard that you just don't wake up in the morning, because you've run out of strength to pretend anymore. I know this wasn't a decision that Brian took lightly and he fought longer and harder than he really had any energy for simply because I asked him to. So even now, after five years, I still have yet to experience the "anger" stage of the grief cycle, and I honestly don't foresee it ever happening. I have felt only compassion for him, because I've felt that despair and wouldn't wish it on anyone, and I certainly wouldn't blame someone for making that choice for him or herself in the end. In fact, I've found myself feeling painfully envious of him for seeking that peace, because I've had so much difficulty finding any of it myself.

I've been writing letters to Brian to express my feelings, and it helps me feel as though I'm talking directly to him and helps me process my thoughts a little more clearly. But every now and then I still fall back on my old habit of self-injury when I'm too overwhelmed to even begin to collect my thoughts and am desperate for a quick release. To anyone who doesn't understand, I'm sure it seems a barbaric ritual (and possibly counterintuitive) to cause oneself physical harm as a means to feel better, but I wouldn't do it if it didn't work. It happens so rarely now but every now and then all the sadness becomes too much to handle and I resort to the ironic "comfort" of the razor blade. It's certainly not ideal, but it helps and for now that's enough for me.

*

MARCELLA MALONE
Marcella's 20-year-old brother
Michael died by suicide in 2014

In the super-emotional state after losing my brother/best friend so suddenly and beginning my third trimester with my first child, yes, I had a few suicidal thoughts. The pain seemed too harsh some moments, and it led to wondering if it would be easier to join Michael, if it would be easier to end my life rather than leave others to deal with the burden of my grief.

The thoughts were not very calculated and rarely lasted more than a couple of hours, but they happened. Consciously I know I couldn't do it, though. I have too much to live for. Just looking into my sons eyes, I know the devastating impact of such a decision.

*

BROOKE NINNI MATTHEWS
Brooke's 31-year-old brother Timothy
died by homicide in 2012

I have thought about suicide after my brother's murder. I was prescribed antidepressants and anxiety medication. I noticed my thoughts of suicide became worse after I started taking the antidepressants. I was then prescribed another brand, but still I was no better. I was just one of those people who they seemed not to help, no matter the brand. I just had to ride out the emotions on my own. It didn't take me long to realize suicide was not the answer to my pain, as my daughter was having thoughts of suicide herself. She was then sent to a child's psychiatric unit for a week and had to attend KidsPeace for four weeks. I knew I had to be strong because she needed me.

*

MICHAEL SMITH
Michael's 39-year-old brother Patrick
was killed by an impaired driver in 2007

Well, no, mainly because now I am the only child remaining to my parents. There have been days that my mind wandered. I don't think I could say it lasted more than five seconds, because I was so intensely angry at the man who caused the crash.

*

DAWN WOINOVICK
Dawn's 52-year-old brother
Todd died from cancer in 2013

There have been times when I felt that people and family would have missed me less than Todd, if I had died instead of him.

CHAPTER TEN

THE FRIENDS

Remember, you don't need a certain number of friends, just a number of friends you can be certain of. -UNKNOWN

When we are mourning, some of our friendships undergo transitions. Some bonds remain steady, dependable and faithful. Some we sever by choice. And, perhaps unexpectedly, new friends enter our life, bringing renewed hope rich with possibilities. But what about your sibling's friends? Do you keep in touch with them?

*

EMILY BAIRD-LEVINE
Emily's 43-year-old brother Don
died from a heart attack in 2004

I have mostly just had interactions with Kitty, Don's fiancée. She is family to me and a huge connection to Don. Don had the best years of his life with Kitty, so the feelings are warm. At first it was hard to talk with Kitty. I felt like I was too much of a reminder of Don. Over time, we came to where we can share good memories and it feels fine. We aren't in touch often, mostly on Don's birthday, on the anniversary of Don's death, on the anniversary of Don's kidney transplant, and to extend greetings for holidays.

*

CHRISTINE BASTONE
Christine's 38-year-old sister
Liz died by suicide in 2012

Sadly I do not really know any of Liz's friends. I did receive a condolence message from one of her previous neighbors. But, because I didn't know the guy, Facebook put it in my "other" folder and I didn't see it for months. I was so upset for a while that such an important message did not go to my inbox. I also very briefly connected with two people whom Liz went to school with.

The only other thing I did in the hopes of connecting with a few of her friends was to write a comment on Liz's MySpace profile saying that she had died. But nobody responded. Although to be fair, they probably didn't see it.

I would absolutely love to connect with some of Liz's friends! It would be so cool to connect with someone who knew her in a slightly different way than I did. And I am sad that so far, at least, I have not been able to do so.

*

SHANNON BOOS
Shannon's 21-year-old brother Kevin
was killed by two drunk drivers in 2015

Kevin and I always had a lot of mutual friends from the time we were young. I am very grateful for this now, because I am still in contact with people who love and miss him as I do.

Something that is upsetting to me, though, is when I feel as though people have moved on, including his friends. It sounds horrible and irrational, and I know it is wrong of me to expect them to grieve and remain in pain forever, but it still hurts. When Kevin was killed, my whole world stopped. It's been a little over a year, and I don't think it has gotten back to turning just yet. So when I see pictures of his groups of friends and he isn't there, I stop and wonder if they wish he were, if they think about him, talk about him, and cry about him just like I still do.

Kevin was the president of Epsilon Sigma Alpha at Florida State University, a fraternity that revolves around community service and outreach. They are a group of people I am very thankful for, and they have made it very clear to my family and me that he has not been forgotten and never will be. On the one-year anniversary of his death, the fraternity held a memorial candle lighting just for him, where people brought flowers and balloons, gave speeches, and shared memories about Kevin.

If I were to tell Kevin's friends something, it would be this: don't forget him. Don't forget our grief. Talk about him, think about him, and cry about him. Share silly little stories or memories with me that you think about during the day. My biggest fear is that the world will forget who Kevin Kyle Boos was, and I spend every day making sure that doesn't happen. And I know a lot of him still lives on in his friends and their memories.

*

LISA FORESTBIRD
Lisa's 40-year-old brother Rob died
from a pontine hemorrhage in 2006

I have maintained a strong relationship with my brother's girlfriend, Molly. Since she is probably more like family, this may be nonresponsive to the question. She has since married and has a child, but we still stay in close touch and often think of our relationship as more like sisters than friends. Her son's favorite stuffed animal is the one I gave him as a baby gift five years ago. While that is probably pretty random, it's still kind of neat. We periodically vacation together and occasionally get lost in phone calls of up to two hours at a time. I live two thousand miles away from where Rob lived, so I don't just run into people or friends who knew him.

*

BONNIE FORSHEY
Bonnie's 54-year-old sister Eunice
died from bladder cancer in 2010

I have spoken to many of my sister's friends and of course they all miss her. One of her friends bought my sister's house. She plans on giving it to my sister's son when he graduates from college. He doesn't know yet, and will be surprised. My sister worked in the local hospital, and everyone knew her. She was also a comedian, and did skits at the hospital performing as Nurse Foxworthy. Her friends have all moved on with their lives. We speak, but no longer go out of our ways to stay in touch.

*

LAURA HABEDANK
Laura's brother Brian died
by suicide in 2010 at age 35

I live so far away from home now that I never see anyone who knew Brian except for during my rare visits home to Minnesota. If I'm being honest, I haven't been back home as often as I probably should, because I'm bombarded with memories when I'm there. It's not as though I have my head buried in the sand about it or anything, because it's still on my mind every day. But I guess those thoughts are a little less overwhelming when I'm not also surrounded by all the places we spent time together and all the people who knew Brian. It's been easier for me to have some distance from all of that and have my very own life here in Texas.

Growing up, our house was where Brian and his best friends hung out nearly all the time, so I basically had a whole extra set of surrogate brothers. It's been hard for me seeing them go through all the amazing changes in adulthood that I haven't had the opportunity to experience with my own brother: getting married, having children and building their dream homes. I'm so happy for them, but there is a part of me that aches because I never got the chance to see these milestones realized for Brian, too.

I will admit there have been moments when I've felt that my attachment to his closest friends has become unhealthy. I miss my brother so much, and they are the closest thing to a brother I have left now. I feel protective of them, but I also feel painfully needy and inferior for reaching out to them like I do at times. This misplaced attachment is not exactly a new phenomenon for me. The first significant death in my life was that of my grandpa, my mom's father, during my senior year in high school. I loved him so much, and was just devastated when he died. At his funeral I became very fixated on his brother, Harold, who was the spitting image of my grandpa. I knew it wasn't him, but Harold looked so much like him that I just stayed glued to his side that day because he was now the closest thing I had left to the real thing. Last month I went home to Minnesota for a visit after not having been there in over two years. I had the chance to see a few of Brian's closest friends, and it meant the world to me to spend time with them and talk about him. To be able to share memories about Brian and know that others miss him too is so precious to me.

*

MARCELLA MALONE
Marcella's 20-year-old brother
Michael died by suicide in 2014

Since Michael's passing, interactions with his friends are very comforting for me. Talking to the people who saw him most during his final couple of years helped me to get to know him better and remember the amazing person he was. Growing up, I became sort of a surrogate big sister to many of Michael's friends. I began to truly care for them and their role in his life. Honestly, I can't imagine not seeing them anymore. It would be like a larger chunk of my life was gone. They help me to remember Michael and manage my grief. While there are a couple of exceptions to this, I love watching them grow. I love being part of their continued existence, despite the sadness it brings me that I will never get to see Michael accomplish the same goals they have.

*

BROOKE NINNI MATTHEWS
Brooke's 31-year-old brother Timothy
died by homicide in 2012

I occasionally have interactions with my brother's friends, and a few of them are friends with me on Facebook. I don't talk to or see any of them other than the few I'm friends with on Facebook. I choose to stay away from the township we grew up in, which is where the murder happened. Many of his friends still live in that township. I can love and keep my brother's memory alive with or without interaction with his friends.

*

NICKI NOBLE
Nicki's 43-year-old brother Don
died from a heart attack in 2004

My sweet brother had lots of friends. He did not live near me nor did his friends. At his memorial it was heartwarming to hear stories of him from their perspective. He was loved by so many. I have not had contact with his friends.

*

BRIDGET PARK
Bridget's brother Austin died
by suicide in 2008 at age 14

My brother's friends and I are now becoming more like friends than acquaintances, because when my brother died I was thirteen and they were all sixteen, so there was quite an age gap. But now that I am older, it is easier to befriend them.

We talk about memories of my brother and how we all miss him. It was nice to hear all their stories and memories, because I can imagine my brother doing these things with them and laughing at these jokes that they are now telling me. It makes me happy to see how loved and missed my brother is, and that he did not leave this earth unnoticed or unloved, but he left this earth along with so many people who cherish him.

*

MICHAEL SMITH
Michael's 39-year-old brother Patrick
was killed by an impaired driver in 2007

Some, mainly one of his girlfriends. She was deeply affected by his death. In fact, I was the one who phoned her and told her it happened. My brother was well liked at his job, the whole crew at Gerber Garment Technology in Tolland, Connecticut, came through for Pat's memory. Since he was killed in December they took the Christmas wish list for Dakota off his workbench, and after taking donations they bought Dakota everything on the list for Christmas.

What amazes me still is how many people came to his wake and funeral, the outpouring of caring and how he had so many friends.

*

DAWN WOINOVICK
Dawn's 52-year-old brother
Todd died from cancer in 2013

We all talk anywhere, any time about Todd, and it always leads to how great of a person he was. Seems like people who die become saints. That's what leads to being alive or not being taken first....guilt comes in. And how much I miss him, like you're not the only one.

*

CHAPTER ELEVEN

THE RELATIONSHIPS

I have found the paradox that if you love until it
hurts, there can be no more hurt, only more love.
-MOTHER TERESA

For many of us, familial relationships are the cornerstones that help us stay sane; they keep us laughing, learning, and loving. We speak one another's language and finish one another's sentences. Sometimes, however, loss of our sibling touches us in different ways. What family relations, if any, were impacted by the loss of your sister or brother?

*

EMILY BAIRD-LEVINE
Emily's 43-year-old brother Don
died from a heart attack in 2004

The relationships most impacted by the loss of my brother are those with my husband and my kids. They have been the ones to see me go through all the phases of grief and the ongoing emotions that crop up as time goes by. They have been there for me and have been supportive through the whole process. I can't imagine it has been easy for them to watch the continued pain of this tremendous loss, and all the while be so understanding of me. I am blessed.

*

CHRISTINE BASTONE
Christine's 38-year-old sister
Liz died by suicide in 2012

Surprisingly the biggest impact has been on my relationship with myself! Oh, I still really dislike the way I look, and some of my circumstances, but deep inside I know that it is what is inside of me that counts. That my presence is valuable, and the people who love me would miss me if I were not here. Because of this I am kinder to myself. Not that all my self-esteem issues have disappeared. But I am grateful that they have improved. And it's all because of how much I miss Liz's presence, and what that taught me.

*

SHANNON BOOS
Shannon's 21-year-old brother Kevin
was killed by two drunk drivers in 2015

All my relationships have been changed in one way or another. Some were tainted with change, others completely shattered. However, in the darkness of the loss of Kevin, some relationships have actually flourished.

Before Kevin died, my relationships with my cousins and my maternal aunts and uncles had been on the rocks. We weren't really talking, and any time we had together was filled with awkwardness and tension. In hindsight, I honestly don't remember much of why things were like this, but that we had just been in a rough patch of our relationships together.

When Kevin died, this changed. And if I have to pick something that I am grateful for (even though I don't like using the term "grateful" when it comes to Kevin's death), it would be how strong my relationships with my cousins, aunts, and uncles have become. We are closer than ever, and I find strength and comfort through the love and hugs I receive from them.

In my opinion, that's how it should be. Any death, but particularly a sudden, traumatic death of a young person like Kevin, should bring people, especially family, together. It should show you how the trivial things in life just don't matter. We should love each other and laugh together, every single day. Because life is so short and so, so fragile.

However, this isn't always the case.

So many relationships in my life have changed dramatically since Kevin was killed, and these changes have easily had some of the most powerful impacts on me in the past year. There were so many people whom I called my best friends whom I have now not heard from in months. I'm sure that when they are confronted, there will be many excuses, but in reality their life has continued and they expect mine to continue as well. I have heard every excuse in the book, such as:

"Sorry, I was busy today." Yet they still have time to post social media pictures and updates, and can't send a quick text message.

"Your grief makes me uncomfortable."

My grief makes you uncomfortable? I'm so sorry that the immense pain I feel is too much for YOU to handle. Next.

"I thought it would be better for you if I left your life."

I'm sorry, what?

When I think of relationships of mine that have been affected, two people come to mind first. These two people were like a second set of parents for me for quite some time, and I even came to love their son who was a baby at the time, more than anything in the world. We had had a falling-out recently before Kevin was killed, but of course I still reached out to them when he died because they had offered a sense of comfort for so long.

They were so incredibly supportive for the first few days. They came to the funeral, called me to check on me, etc. But then their world kept going, and mine was expected to start turning again too. Their true colors were always right in front of me to see, but I really didn't get a clear view of them until my phone calls and text messages went unanswered two weeks after the funeral of my brother.

I have finally learned to accept that anyone who is a true friend of mine would not have an excuse. Sadly, I can only count my true friends on one hand at this point in time.

This is how it happens. Your loved one dies. There's a funeral. Hundreds of people show up. Hundreds of hugs and offers of condolences. You start to think, wow. Maybe I can do this. Maybe I can get through this. These people surround you with so much love and support that it makes all the scary, heartbreaking parts of his death blurry.

But in reality, these people go to a funeral, and they go home. That's it. Time to get on with their lives. They don't have time for you or your pain. They expect you to just pick up and keep moving. Of course, in some cases I'm sure this is possible for some people. Maybe when it is an older loved one, someone who is sick, dying, or in pain, and they pass, of course it hurts. But maybe you can feel some sort of relief that they are "in a better place."

However, when your twenty-one-year-old brother is killed by a drunk driver with two of his friends, and people try to tell you that he's in a better place, it's a smack to the face.

He's in a better place? Where? Can I go? Because I'm pretty sure that there is no better place than here with our family and me.

He wasn't sick. He wasn't in pain. He was killed. Murdered. Gone in a second.

Then you have the friends who don't understand why you haven't moved on. Frankly, it has been over a year and I still haven't "moved on." I still cry about Kevin. Mostly in private, but I still do.

I remember one moment in particular. A friend (I honestly don't remember who it was) had come to me for advice. It hadn't even been a month since Kevin was killed, and she had come to me asking for a shoulder to cry on because of some sort of "boy issues" she was having.

I very politely explained that I was in no place to offer her any sort of advice or comfort because I was still lacking any sort of relief for my own pain.

This started a huge argument that ended with this friend calling me selfish for not helping her with her problems. But I was too caught up in my own.

This friend was in effect asking me to help her with her stubbed toe while I couldn't find half of my body.

I still to this day struggle to understand the logic and thought that went into the words and actions (or lack of them) that I heard and saw from my friends, and even some of my family. I feel as though if my friend had lost someone so traumatically, I would do anything and everything I could to help, and to be there. If I wasn't sure what to do, I would ask. But I try to give the benefit of the doubt, because I've never been on that side of all of this.

I don't hear from a lot of my old friends anymore. And I guess that's okay. Because I have narrowed down my group of friends to those who truly care and want to help me through this horrible, horrible "journey." At the end of the day, I learned a lot about these people. They weren't ever really my friends. Anyone who truly loves and cares about me would be there. No questions asked. No excuses. And some were, and still are. And I am so grateful.

If I could offer any sort of advice to a friend of a bereaved person who may be reading this, it would be this: speak up. Talk to your friend. Ask how they are. Talk about their loved one(s). Ask about them. Tell stories about them. Because I promise you, the amount of discomfort you feel about the situation, it does not even compare to the amount of pain your friend is feeling. And he or she hasn't moved on, hasn't forgotten.

It astounds me how quiet my phone has gotten over the past year, especially on holidays and Kevin's birthday and anniversaries of his death. I think that people assume that my family and I have moved on, or we don't want to hear from anyone. But they are so wrong. I've even called people out on this, whether it is privately or on a rant on social media. But there are still people who refuse to speak up. And I will never, ever understand that.

*

LISA FORESTBIRD
Lisa's 40-year-old brother Rob died
from a pontine hemorrhage in 2006

I do not believe losing Rob caused any close relationships to become strained.

*

BONNIE FORSHEY
Bonnie's 54-year-old sister Eunice
died from bladder cancer in 2010

The loss of my sister has created temporary disconnects with her children. My niece moved to Hawaii, a nephew moved to Lock Haven, Pennsylvania, to attend college, and the youngest nephew was taken to Texas to live with his father. They all went in different directions and I never get to see them now. My sister held everything together when she was here.

*

LAURA HABEDANK
Laura's brother Brian died
by suicide in 2010 at age 35

I think it's absolutely true that you genuinely find out who your real friends are when tragedy strikes. I had friends who I was certain would be there for me who virtually disappeared, and that hurt more than you could imagine. As if the suicide of my only sibling wasn't hard enough, I lost friends because they couldn't handle my grief or just didn't know what to say to me.

But I also gained some new friends and experienced a regeneration of friendships that had dissipated over the years; I had people I hadn't heard from in years reach out to me in unbelievably kind ways. A childhood friend whom I hadn't seen in probably ten years started calling me every week. Since I was still in my "I just can't answer the phone" phase, she left me a voicemail each time she called. She would simply say, "I know you probably don't feel like talking, and that is totally okay. Please just know that I'm thinking of you and I'm here if you want to talk; don't feel pressured to call me back, I'll completely understand if you're not ready. I love you and I'm thinking about you." I can't think of a more loving and selfless thing for a friend to do at a time like that — just to reach out to let me know I was loved but at the same time not being upset with me for not having the strength to reach back.

I had been married for six years when Brian died, and my marriage had already been struggling for a while. Just eleven months earlier we had moved to Texas from my home state of Minnesota, and the stress of that move and the loss of having my close friends around me had taken a toll on me and on my marriage, because a big part of me resented my husband for wanting that drastic move so badly. He already had friends and family here, so he had a built-in support system in place when we relocated.

I had already made wonderful friends here in Texas by the time Brian passed, which was a huge help to me because my relationship with my husband only continued to grow increasingly distant. He wanted the old me back and was so deeply angry at Brian for ending his own life; my husband absolutely hated how it had destroyed my spirit. As a result, I didn't feel comfortable showing my grief around him, because I didn't want to contribute to his feelings of anger at Brian; I didn't want anyone to be upset with someone I loved so much. So I did most of my crying alone, and numbed the pain with wine and weed nearly every night.

Our relationship continued to deteriorate, and just over half a year after Brian's death we filed for divorce. It was a completely respectful, loving, and amicable divorce, and we parted as friends. A huge part of me was so relieved because the divorce was a new start for me, and I was so relieved to have the space to just work on myself and let my grief take any shape and form that it needed to without the judgment of my spouse or the pressure I put on myself to keep it together for his sake.

My parents have also since divorced. I wouldn't say that Brian's death had anything to do with it, because their marriage had been so strained for so very long but I'm sure it didn't help either. Everyone grieves differently, and I am certain that couples, when they lose a child, either grow closer together or drift farther apart. My dad has rarely spoken about my brother since Brian's death, and seems to have internalized the loss, because outwardly he doesn't seem to be grieving at all. He has even referred to me as an only child, which is so painful because I don't consider myself an only child at all. I have a sibling. I'm a sister to a deceased brother. I haven't spoken to him about my anger about that, because I have every bit of hope that maybe he just can't express his grief. But that disparity has certainly driven another wedge in our already strained relationship. I'm sure that was hard on my mom, too.

My relationship with my mom has changed in a lot of ways, but the most pronounced way is the sense of pressure I now feel. I'm all she has left now, so I know how much she worries and panics when she can't reach me, or when I get sick, or worse, when I suffer another deep, depressive episode.

*

MARCELLA MALONE
Marcella's 20-year-old brother
Michael died by suicide in 2014

There is nothing like the loss of someone so close to you to affect the relationships in your life, especially with those who might not have known Michael well, or at all. The relationship between my boyfriend and me has suffered the most since Michael's death. Our pregnancy happened accidentally, and very early in our relationship. My boyfriend had a chance to meet my brother only twice, for a few hours. He didn't get a chance to know him or the strength of the bond between us. Despite that, he was the one I had to lean on.

After a short week with my family, I went home to him. He was the one I woke up to after having nightmares, the one who had to pick me up off the floor when I was weak or collapsed in tears, the one who got the short end of the stick when I was angry over what I didn't know, and the one who had to meet the other half of his son's family under such terrible circumstances. On most days my boyfriend was great about being there for me, but some days it was too much for him. We fought and barely survived as a couple a time or two. Not having a strong family or having known mine, he truly didn't understand my pain, and we took it out on each other. While we still have our down moments, surviving the biggest tragedy of my life together has made our relationship stronger than ever.

The other relationship that has suffered a lot of strain since the loss of Michael is that with my parents. We still have a strong relationship and tell each other almost everything, but it's different now. We talk little about what happened and largely leave out our emotions regarding it. I'm not comfortable sharing my feelings and struggles with them, as I know they are suffering much worse. Sometimes it's hard to leave this out, but I can't bring myself to do it. I also caught myself putting part of the blame for what happened on them, and I can't forgive myself for these thoughts. I love them too much.

*

BROOKE NINNI MATTHEWS
Brooke's 31-year-old brother Timothy
died by homicide in 2012

I did disconnect with a few family members and friends because of the loss. Most of the disconnect happened through social media. They didn't like that I was always posting photos of and memories about my brother, and they didn't like that I was always posting messages to him on his social media account. They couldn't handle or didn't understand why I just couldn't get over my brother's murder. My brother was a huge part of my life and a sibling is supposed to grow old with you. He was my brother and alive or dead, I will always think of him every day, as I do my other siblings.

*

NICKI NOBLE
Nicki's 43-year-old brother Don
died from a heart attack in 2004

I would say that the relationship most impacted, because it became strained, was with my brother's sweet fiancée. She lost her soul mate. She told me a number of times that she felt responsible to some degree because she didn't feel she was able to perform CPR fast enough. I completely disagree. Don was on borrowed time for quite a while. There was nothing anyone could have done. The strain on our relationship stems from, I believe, the fact that she was someone very special to my sweet brother. Perhaps she felt it would be too painful to continue a relationship with us, with all those memories and plans of what would have been had Don lived. I have included his fiancée in numerous family events, and contact with her has been met with mixed response. She has a very demanding career so I understand. She also does not live close by. I am at a loss sometimes on how to approach her. However, the last time I saw her, we had a heartwarming chat that included tears and laughter. It has been ten years and I worry about her. I know my sweet brother would want her to find someone else, and have a happy life.

*

BRIDGET PARK
Bridget's brother Austin died
by suicide in 2008 at age 14

My father and I had a lot of stress on our relationship after my brother's suicide. My mother was very comforting to me because her older brother died by suicide as well when she was also only a teenager. My dad felt very guilty because he thought that he was too hard on my brother, and that he never cut him any slack. My parents had really high expectations for my brother and me, and we were held to a high standard at all times. Some may think that this is a good thing, but I don't think my brother handled it as well as I did. My dad was especially harder on my brother than he was on me, because he was two years older than me. My dad disappeared from my life emotionally and mentally when my brother passed. When my dad was around my mother and me, he was never fully present. It was like "the lights were on but nobody's home" kind of look. My dad was also on a lot of different kinds of antidepressants after my brother passed, which often made him seem loopy and intoxicated. I think my dad took my brother's death harder than the rest of us and showed more signs of grief than the rest of us did.

It was very difficult for me to see my father in this state, but it also made me angry at him. He would miss my volleyball games or school events, because he was at work or simply forgot, whereas beforehand he had always made it a priority to go to my games and events. I know that my dad did not mean to hurt or disappoint me, but it was inevitable for me to feel this way. My dad focused so much on the fact that he lost a child, but he forgot and neglected the fact that he still has a daughter who was alive and needed her father. My mother was very sympathetic to me and tried to compensate for my dad's absence, and I really appreciate my mother in that way.

This phase lasted for two to three years, and soon Dad was able to clear his head and heart. I do not resent my dad for this, because I know that he did not want to hurt me and that he was hurting.

*

MICHAEL SMITH
Michael's 39-year-old brother Patrick
was killed by an impaired driver in 2007

It began a slow disconnect with my partner of many years. We were not in the best place anyway, and the amount of focus I spent trying to obtain information and force the State of Connecticut to do something about my brother's death drove a wedge between us. My performance at work decreased, and my interaction with other people began to fade, as I was no longer interested in going anywhere or doing anything.

*

DAWN WOINOVICK
Dawn's 52-year-old brother
Todd died from cancer in 2013

My relationship with my folks has been most impacted in both a negative and positive way. At first we supported each other as a family circle as Todd's cancer crashed around us. For weeks we all rallied around Todd, to take care of him at home with hospice care. Spending as much time together as we could even to the point of arguing over who could do what. When Todd stopped communication in his final few days, he expressed his frustration with our behavior. At times it was tough. When Todd took his last breath, our world crashed. We all retreated and went through the motions. They let me be a part of everything, but I felt like an outsider. I even felt guilty that I was alive. Over time our relationship has found a new normal but will forever never be what it once was.

*

CHAPTER TWELVE

THE FAITH

Love is the only law capable of transforming grief
into hope. -LYNDA CHELDELIN FELL

Grief has far-reaching effects in most areas of our life, including faith. For some, our faith can deepen as it becomes a safe haven for our sorrow. For others, it can be a source of disappointment, leading to fractured beliefs. One commonality among the bereaved is that faith is often altered one way or the other. Has your faith or belief system been impacted by your loss?

*

EMILY BAIRD-LEVINE
Emily's 43-year-old brother Don
died from a heart attack in 2004

I haven't ever been a very observant Jew, but prior to Don's passing I did embrace Judaism to some degree within my immediate family. We would have a nice dinner for Shabbat on Friday nights, light candles, say blessings over bread and wine and grape juice. After Don died, I couldn't bring myself to do any of these rituals. They suddenly seemed to lack meaning to me. I questioned any iota of belief I had begun to acquire over the years. It wasn't until years after losing Don that I was able to start doing some of the minimal things I had done previously. I have continued most years to observe the anniversary of Don's death in the traditional Jewish way. I don't know if that brings me the comfort I would hope for. Most people observe the anniversary of the passing of a parent and not the passing of a sibling. I feel isolated in the process. I like that the prayer that is recited is a celebration of life, not specifically of loss. Even still it is a ritual, although somewhat helpful, that still leaves a void for me.

*

CHRISTINE BASTONE
Christine's 38-year-old sister
Liz died by suicide in 2012

My loss made me question almost everything I have ever believed, and has also drastically changed what I believe.

I clearly remember being in the library looking for books that might help me in my grief. I picked up one written by a medium, *We Are Their Heaven,* by Allison DuBois. I was always taught that mediums are a big no-no, so I put it back. But then I decided that my sister's death was causing me enough pain to read such a book anyway. And so I checked it out. I devoured it, and any other book that I can find written by a medium. I have since come to believe that it is only fake mediums who are a no-no.

After my sister died, I began to wonder what part of what I had believed was of God, and what part was only of man. One of the biggest changes is how I feel about the Bible. The original translation of the Bible is not English. Men have translated it. I believe that at least sometimes there is something missing, or maybe even inaccurate with the translation. So I no longer take it as the final authority on everything.

140

I also no longer oppose gay marriage. I no longer oppose gay people period, and I wish that they, along with everyone else, were welcomed with open arms at all churches.

I can no longer fathom God sending anyone to hell. I believe that Christ died to save all of us, not just a few who accept Him. I believe that hell is much more likely to frequently be here and now, and not after we die. I believe that only demons and the devil deserve hell. I do, however, believe in different levels of heaven. I also believe that we will all go through some sort of life review.

I still consider myself a Christian. I'm just no longer a fundamental Christian. I find myself being ashamed of how many other Christians treat people who are grieving and people who are survivors of a suicide attempt or of a suicide loss. I even find myself ashamed of how many Christians treat people who are different than they have been taught that people should be such as people who are divorced, living together without marriage, or are gay. In my spiritual search, I ended up finding out about how much abuse goes on in way too many churches, not that it would be acceptable for it to happen even in just one church. But even the way too many churches treat women is just awful. Not that that's the point here, but as a fellow Christian, I have been horrified and ashamed of that. Telling anyone that his or her loved one is in hell is never a Christian thing to do. Giving simplistic advice such as "All you need to do is pray and read the Bible" isn't helpful either. Judging people is no less a sin than the very things that so many Christians judge people for. And I wish they would realize that.

People are supposed to know we are Christians by our love. And too many Christians are known by their hate instead. In the support groups I belong to, I have heard so many times how much anguish is caused by many comments that too many Christians make. It makes me angry on their behalf. I just want to hug them, and tell them that not all Christians are like that. So yes, my faith was greatly impacted by my loss. And while I know many people won't agree with me, I think it was an impact for the better.

*

SHANNON BOOS
Shannon's 21-year-old brother Kevin
was killed by two drunk drivers in 2015

I was raised in a Catholic home because my mother has always been very religious. My father, not so much, but nonetheless, my brothers and I were taken to church every Sunday. As I got older, I started to drift away from the religion for many reasons. Anytime something painful would happen to me, one of my first thoughts would be if there is a God, why do things like this happen?

When Kevin was killed, this question still popped into my head. I cannot think of any reason why God would take my brother and our two friends like that. To be killed in such a senseless way, so quickly and so traumatically.

I always tried to believe that everything happens for a reason. In some cases, I do believe it is true. For instance, when I was in high school my dream college was the University of Florida. After all my hard work, I was rejected by the school. I was absolutely devastated. I ended up attending Florida State University, my second choice school, for two years with Kevin and my two friends Morgan and Cenzo by my side. If I had been accepted into UF, I would have lost two amazing years with my three angels, so that is something I believe happened for a reason. However there is absolutely no reason that the three of them had to be killed. If you try to feed me this, I won't believe you. I don't know if there is a God. But if there is, I don't ever want to know him.

142

*

LISA FORESTBIRD
Lisa's 40-year-old brother Rob died
from a pontine hemorrhage in 2006

Not really. I used my faith as a coping mechanism. I feel that losing Rob must be part of the master plan.

*

BONNIE FORSHEY
Bonnie's 54-year-old sister Eunice
died from bladder cancer in 2010

I am no longer religious, just spiritual.

*

LAURA HABEDANK
Laura's brother Brian died
by suicide in 2010 at age 35

The issue of "faith" is kind of a tricky one for me. I was raised going to church, and became increasingly active in my youth group in junior high and high school. However, the older I got and the more I learned about all kinds of other religions, the less sense *any* of them made to me. I decided years ago that I don't believe we were created by a heavenly being in the sky. I do, however, believe that we are all made of energy and are connected, and that after death a part of us lives on in some form.

Some of the more hurtful things I've heard numerous times since Brian's suicide include: "It was God's will," or "God needed another angel," or "He's with Jesus now," or "God doesn't give you more than you can handle." I wish that people wouldn't be so quick to assume that I share their beliefs, because those statements did me more harm than good. And after my father attempted suicide in

1995, a born-again Christian friend of mine, instead of simply saying, "I'm sorry that happened, I hope he's okay now," he chose to proclaim to me that my dad would be spending an eternity burning in hell for committing the ultimate sin. To date, that is still one of the most uncaring and heartless things anyone ever said to me. I don't see the point of saying something like that to another human being who is hurting.

While I don't believe in the idea of heaven or hell, I do believe that our spirits continue in some shape or form. I've felt that way for quite some time, even long before Brian's death. But just six weeks after he died, I had the most amazing experience, and I'm positive that Brian visited me in a dream. In this dream, Mom and I were in some house, I believe it was supposed to be Brian's place, although everything looked so different. I heard his voice, very groggy, as though he were just waking up. He was calling my name, saying "Laura...., Laura....it's Brian." I was frantically looking around, thinking there was no way I could have just heard what I thought I heard. I ran down the stairs, and as I approached the last few steps I saw Brian walking toward me. For some reason he was carrying an oxygen tank and had a breathing tube going to his nose. I sat down on the bottom few steps with Mom sitting just a few steps behind me. As Brian stood on the floor next to the staircase, he took both my hands in his. I thought to myself, "There is no way this is happening; could he really be here with us now?" I glanced up at Mom and cried as I asked her, "Mom, what is happening?" I needed to see if she was hearing and seeing what I was, and she assured me that she was. However, I sensed from her that it didn't mean that he was alive. I looked at Brian again and he looked really good. He looked so peaceful and rested and happy. He had that pink glow back in his cheeks, and his eyes told me he was okay. I asked him how he was and he said, "I'm all right now.

I was cured the moment I passed away. I love you very much and I miss you." I told him that I loved him and missed him too, and hugged him and cried. I kept looking at Mom to see if she was hearing it, and she kept assuring me that she was. But she stayed there quietly next to me and just watched and listened, as if she knew that this moment with Brian was meant just for me.

Then Mom and I were saying our goodbyes downstairs to Brian as if we were leaving his place like any other time before. Mom asked, "Are you going to be okay? What are you going to do now?" He said, "I'm good. I'm going to just run out for a bit." He had a cup of coffee in one hand and reached for his car keys with the other, as if he were truly only going to hop into his red Saturn and go for a drive. That's the thing last I remember before waking up. I woke up feeling so peaceful and grateful that I'd had that dream. I believed then, and still believe today, that it was my brother reaching out to let me know he wasn't suffering anymore. It was the most unbelievably moving experience of my life.

Brian wasn't a religious person either. I chose beautiful, non-religious writings to be included in the funeral service. We also chose to include a poem that Grandpa Ralph had written not long before his own death in 2003:

> *If you happen to think of me*
> *Remember how I used to be.*
> *And when, while you're pausing,*
> *After I am laid to rest,*
> *Take a moment to recall*
> *That of me that was best.*

I thought this poem particularly fitting, as I want Brian to be remembered for his life and his loving spirit, not for the manner in which he died, because there was so much more to him that those who loved him were lucky enough to experience. And there is not a single part of me that will ever believe there is a god out there somewhere who sent my brother's soul to some kind of eternal, fiery hell for giving up.

*

MARCELLA MALONE
Marcella's 20-year-old brother
Michael died by suicide in 2014

I have always been a nondenominational Christian. Growing up, I always attended church, was in youth group, worked in the church nursery, taught children's church, etc. The farther I got into college, the less I attended church or did anything with this aspect of my life. After Michael's death, I found great comfort in thoughts of heaven and the prospect of seeing him again one day. This brought me to finding a church to attend that was near my new home, and making the decision to raise my child in a church. While my relationship with my faith was strengthened, I have also found that I am more skeptical of what I hear, am more emotional toward certain topics, and have to deal with my anger toward God for taking away my brother. My faith has been a rollercoaster since Michael's death, with my comfort always being in heaven and my belief that suicide does not keep you out of it.

*

BROOKE NINNI MATTHEWS
Brooke's 31-year-old brother Timothy
died by homicide in 2012

Absolutely has! I used to believe you had to have a religion, but I don't believe that to be true anymore. When I lost my brother to murder, I didn't study or read the Bible like most do when they've lost a loved one. I started studying and learning more about the afterlife and spirit world. I believe there is life after death, or shall I say, there is no such thing as death. I believe we shed our physical bodies and our soul lives on in a higher dimension, and each soul vibrates at a different level, there is no hell. We are all children of God, he is in all of us, and he loves us all, therefore, I don't believe he would send us to a place like hell. I understand everyone has their own religion and belief, this is just mine.

*

NICKI NOBLE
Nicki's 43-year-old brother Don
died from a heart attack in 2004

I am not a spiritual or religious person, so no.

*

BRIDGET PARK
Bridget's brother Austin died
by suicide in 2008 at age 14

My faith increased drastically when my brother passed. I was only twelve when he passed, and before his death I never had any traumatic events that I really needed to lean on my faith for.

I really leaned on faith and the fact that my brother was in fact in heaven and that his spirit was with us every day. I am Catholic so only about a decade ago, suicide was still considered to be a mortal sin, meaning that one can go to hell for this. I do not agree with this teaching but thankfully the church has reformed it. At my brother's funeral our priest spoke of forgiveness and unconditional love that God has for us, which was very comforting to hear and get reassurance that my brother will go to heaven.

Despite this, there was a phase when I was angry at God and did not understand why He couldn't save my brother from his terrible mistake. He performs medical miracles every day and I struggled with the question of why he did not save my brother and keep him alive. I was angry that my brother was not worthy of God's grace because God did not step in and save his life.

I became very angry and resentful toward God and I questioned His ability. I questioned if there was a point when science overrules miracles and if there was any possible way for God to do anything to help my brother. Since Austin shot himself and it happened so fast, was God not prepared to save him or was the wound too severe? I was very indifferent to my faith at this point, and ignored it for about a year. I finally came to peace with this about a year ago and I have seen my faith grow ever since. I am not as religious as I was when I was living back at home with my parents, but I have seen my faith grow and have seen that I have been relying on it more now that I am an adult.

*

MICHAEL SMITH
Michael's 39-year-old brother Patrick
was killed by an impaired driver in 2007

Yes, my faith was impacted. I didn't understand how a god could possibly let such a good person suffer such a horrible death.

*

DAWN WOINOVICK
Dawn's 52-year-old brother
Todd died from cancer in 2013

My faith, due to so many other situations and circumstances of my life, has been a very strong one. But I lost my brother and friend, the person who knew all of me on an earthly level all my life. The person I fought with, tattled on, told my secrets to, dated his friends, the guy who dated my girlfriends. The pain in the butt older brother who lied all the time and got me in so much trouble for stuff I never did.

Yeah, my faith was impacted because Todd and I talked during his last weeks about God and he asked me if I thought God would ever forgive him for all the things he'd done in his life. In tears, I told Todd that yes. I shared with him how to go to God and how to ask Jesus into his life. At the time I felt relief for him. As the days progressed and he could no longer speak, I did bless him with last rights in the name of the Father, the Son, and the Holy Spirit. A day and half later the Lord led Todd home in peace. Yes, my life was very much impacted. I am an ordained pastor and look forward to seeing my brother in heaven one day.

*

I loved performing; I was always trying
to impress my siblings by being a clown.
I think that came from being the runt of the litter.

ROSE BYRNE

*

CHAPTER THIRTEEN

OUR HEALTH

Health is a state of complete physical, mental, and
social well-being. -WORLD HEALTH ORGANIZATION

As our anatomical and physiological systems work in tandem with
our emotional well-being, when one part of our body is stressed,
other parts become compromised. For some, grief leads to a total
disregard of all health habits while others embrace improved habits
to help strengthen coping abilities. Has your grief affected your
physical health?

*

EMILY BAIRD-LEVINE
Emily's 43-year-old brother Don
died from a heart attack in 2004

When Don first passed away, my health declined a bit due to a
lack of appetite, lack of sleep, shock, trauma, and lack of joy. I lost
weight I didn't need to lose, and I was less physically active.
As time went on, losing my brother has motivated me to take better
care of myself. I have, most of my life been aware of the importance
of eating right, so that continues. I also have a good exercise
routine. Being diagnosed with type I diabetes as an adult, and

through Don I have watched how diabetes can affect so many aspects of one's health. I have made it a priority to do whatever I can to keep my blood sugar under the best possible control, to hopefully minimize complications over time.

*

CHRISTINE BASTONE
Christine's 38-year-old sister
Liz died by suicide in 2012

I already had chronic fatigue syndrome for a long time before my loss. That being said, grief is very exhausting. I think that it has increased the exhaustion that I already feel on a daily basis. And of course it certainly hasn't improved my health any.

*

SHANNON BOOS
Shannon's 21-year-old brother Kevin
was killed by two drunk drivers in 2015

Before Kevin, Vincenzo, and Morgan were killed I was very healthy. I was at a great weight, and very physically active. However, when they died I did change physically over time.

I used to go to the gym several times a week, and I also used to go for runs fairly regularly. After September 6, 2015, that all changed. I didn't care about anything anymore, including myself. I barely moved, I barely slept. It wasn't so much what I was eating that was the issue, it was that I wasn't moving to work it off or stay balanced.

In about six months I gained about forty pounds.

There are some days when I can't even look at myself in the mirror. Family and friends get annoyed with me because I hate

152

myself in pictures and they either need to be retaken or just not posted on any form of social media. There are some days when I am able to love myself and my body, but they come rarely.

I do miss my old body and my old confidence. But I have learned to be patient with myself and understand that the important thing is that I am alive and breathing and hanging in there.

It's been a year, and I am finally starting to become physically healthy again. I am starting to work toward a better me with a higher confidence, and trying to learn that the number on the scale is just a number. I am still here and living for my brother, and that is what is important. Not swimsuit season.

*

LISA FORESTBIRD
Lisa's 40-year-old brother Rob died
from a pontine hemorrhage in 2006

I have not except ever since Rob passed away I sleep eight hours per night. I needed more sleep after Rob passed away and got into the habit of sleeping more, and now it's hard to go back.

*

BONNIE FORSHEY
Bonnie's 54-year-old sister Eunice
died from bladder cancer in 2010

My health has been declining since then. I miss my sister, she has always been in my life. We talked about everything and now I am left with a huge void in my life.

*

LAURA HABEDANK
Laura's brother Brian died
by suicide in 2010 at age 35

In the five years since Brian's death I have gained forty pounds, and honestly I don't feel healthy at all. My energy level is still poor, though I do get out for the occasional hike. I'm completely aware that my self-soothing by way of a lot of wine and pretty much anything and everything that I feel like eating has caused the decline in my physical health. I know something needs to change, but for now I just don't have the energy to do much about it.

It angers me when people preach to me about depression and how "if you'd just eat better and exercise, it would help you so much with your mood." At my healthiest, I was running fifty to sixty miles a week, eating well, I consumed no caffeine or alcohol yet I was deeply depressed, feeling suicidal and self-injuring multiple times a day. I'd never argue that exercise and a healthy diet aren't good for you, because they absolutely are. But they aren't a treatment for clinical depression.

Even at that healthy weight and having enough energy to get up at 5:30 a.m. and run twelve miles before work, I still hated my body, felt insecure and hopeless. It wasn't until I was put on medication that I noticed an improvement in my mood. That was fifteen years ago, and I'm still on medication today, though I go to my psychiatrist multiple times a year to stay on top of the dosage.

I recall Brian and I having a conversation before he died about physical health in relation to depression, too. In 2004, Brian entered his first bodybuilding competition, and I was so impressed with all his hard work. In addition to working full time he was also going to school, had a part-time weekend job, and did all his training for the competition alone. He studied up on it a great deal and was so impressively diligent about sticking to a strict diet and lifting routine, and his physique changed in a startling way. He confided in me that he had found himself over-exercising often as a way to distract himself from his feelings of depression, and it became an unhealthy addiction of sorts. I shared with him that I felt the same way about all my running; I began to use it as a coping mechanism that became an obsession. In addition to all the cutting I was doing, each time I was feeling depressed or anxious I would throw on my running shoes and go run anywhere from six to nine miles multiple times a day! I realized I was using it as a distraction from my feelings.

It made me realize that when you're that depressed, anything can become an unhealthy pastime if abused. I reached an unhealthily low weight, and it concerned me and it concerned those who loved me. Sadly, I've now swung back to the other side of the pendulum and am painfully aware that my body isn't so happy with the choices I've been making for myself lately; that's something I definitely need to work on.

*

MARCELLA MALONE
Marcella's 20-year-old brother
Michael died by suicide in 2014

For the first year or so after my brother's death, I became less interested in being healthy and getting into shape. I had spent the previous year working on this and was in the best shape and at the lowest weight I had been since middle school, despite being seven months pregnant. After Michael's death I felt no motivation to continue and became rather lazy. Through the first year after my son's birth I gained twenty-five pounds. In the last month or so I have just gotten back to getting healthy again, but I am barely able to run a mile. With his birthday coming up in less than two weeks, I catch myself slipping back into a rut. I need to keep reminding myself to change before it causes more health problems for the sake of being around for my child. Grief definitely makes health a larger struggle for me.

*

BROOKE NINNI MATTHEWS
Brooke's 31-year-old brother Timothy
died by homicide in 2012

When I lost my brother to murder, I have since suffered from depression and anxiety, as does my twelve-year-old daughter. She suffered from depression and extreme anxiety to the point where she was admitted to a child's psychiatric unit in 2013 for a week.

*

NICKI NOBLE
Nicki's 43-year-old brother Don
died from a heart attack in 2004

For about two years after my sweet brother passed away, I was having trouble sleeping. I cried often, was very stressed and oh, so sad. I am doing better now but still have my moments.

*

MARYELLEN ROACH
MaryEllen's 41-year-old sister Suzette
died in a car accident in 2012

I was diagnosed with fibromyalgia about seven years ago and many of the symptoms were already prominent, but they have become much, much worse since Suzette moved to heaven. The symptoms that affect my life are constant pain, stiffness, fatigue, concentration and memory issues, anxiety, depression, sleep problems, numbness in my hands, spider veins in my legs, gum and tooth sensitivity, sensitivity to loud noise, sensory overload, mood swings, and the list goes on.

I also attended counseling for several months after the accident and was diagnosed with an anxiety disorder, posttraumatic stress disorder, and major depressive disorder. The symptoms I experience every minute of every day make life hard in general and it also makes handling grief more difficult. The combination of grief and fibromyalgia is like a vicious circle; when grief is in the forefront for the moment, more intense fibromyalgia symptoms are not far behind. When the fibromyalgia symptoms are more front and center, it breaks down my endurance, further limits activities I can do and makes me feel more depressed which then allows the grief and anxiety to creep in, even more than usual.

*

MICHAEL SMITH
Michael's 39-year-old brother Patrick
was killed by an impaired driver in 2007

My eating sleeping and other health issues have definitely been affected. I stayed up all hours of the night for months at a time to research other accidents with impaired diabetics and still maintain a job didn't help my health. That covers physical health.

Mentally, however, I most definitely have suffered a lack of healthy well-being. I have been preoccupied for so many years about this whole event that I've pretty much let many issues of my health slide, including being with friends, going places, and just in general being somewhat housebound.

*

DAWN WOINOVICK
Dawn's 52-year-old brother
Todd died from cancer in 2013

Yes, everything changes. Grief has a way of knocking you to your knees. I believe your immune system has a response as well as your whole being. Its seems to me that every fiber of our being grieves, if we are honest with ourselves. When your muscles tingle, cry and see if that doesn't bring you some relief. When your heart is bothering you, try journaling how you feel. I'll bet you that the pain might just ease up.

I now have fibromyalgia. I never had it before and, to be honest, I never thought it was real. But guess what: it's real. Unresolved issues maybe? Still trying to figure it out. Or could it be that my body finally hit an overload? So many things have happened to me in life, maybe this was the straw that broke the camel's back so to speak. Or I'll just keep trying to understand my mind, my body, my heart, my emotions, and me.

*

CHAPTER FOURTEEN

THE QUIET

Heavy hearts, like heavy clouds in the sky, are best relieved by the letting go of a little water. -ANTOINE RIVAROL

The endless void left in our sister's or brother's absence remains day and night. When our minds are free from distractions there is a moment when sorrow fills the void, threatening to overtake us, unleashing the torrent of tears. For some, that moment happens during the day, for others it comes at night. What time is hardest for you?

*

EMILY BAIRD-LEVINE
Emily's 43-year-old brother Don
died from a heart attack in 2004

Nighttime and sleep time were the hardest times for several months after Don died. This is that quiet, alone, introspective time when I would get flooded with replaying all of the events leading up to his death. If I was able to fall asleep, I would soon wake up startled, panicked, crying, reliving, and hoping that it was all a nightmare and I was going to wake up from it and the reality would somehow differ.

As the years passed, nights haven't been so bad. I can sleep. The replaying of events can happen at any time and the streams of tears flow for known reasons and unknown reasons. I have learned to just let them be and not fight them or hide them.

*

CHRISTINE BASTONE
Christine's 38-year-old sister
Liz died by suicide in 2012

For a long time my hardest time of day was between 7:30 p.m. until around 10 p.m. You see, my parents called me a little after 8 p.m. on that fateful day that I learned Liz had died. And so any time the phone rang around that same time, I would automatically panic. This went on for at least a year. Thankfully, ever since a good friend of mine starting calling me a lot around that same time, that panic lessened a bit. Since I knew it was likely to be my friend who was calling, I was able to relax to a large degree. But I still feel at least a twinge of that fear every time the phone rings during the evening.

*

SHANNON BOOS
Shannon's 21-year-old brother Kevin
was killed by two drunk drivers in 2015

First thing in the morning. Right when I would open my eyes. That was definitely the hardest.

I dream about Kevin often. Sometimes they're pleasant dreams, sometimes they're horrible nightmares. However, in the first few weeks after he was killed I dreamed of him every single night. Whether it was a good dream or a nightmare, my eyes would fly open. It would take a few seconds, maybe ten, to determine what parts of my dream were real and which weren't. But at the end of my relay of events, every single time, the part about his being alive was not real, and the part of him being dead was.

This was awful. When I was asleep, it was an escape from reality. I didn't have to worry about anything; I didn't have to control anything. I could escape. And I would sleep often, at least fourteen hours a day. Waking up snapped me back into reality. The realization that Kevin was gone would knock the wind out of me with no mercy, no second thought.

Wake up, your brother is still dead.

*

LISA FORESTBIRD
Lisa's 40-year-old brother Rob died
from a pontine hemorrhage in 2006

Probably once it started to get dark. It just reminded me of what sometimes felt like a big, dark, and lonely world.

*

BONNIE FORSHEY
Bonnie's 54-year-old sister Eunice
died from bladder cancer in 2010

I miss her all of the time, but mornings are the hardest. She used to call me every morning to see how I was, and to see if I wanted to go shopping with her. She took me to my doctor appointments and later, I took her to hers.

*

LAURA HABEDANK
Laura's brother Brian died
by suicide in 2010 at age 35

In the beginning, mornings were the hardest for me mostly

because I was always so tired from night after night of restless sleep. But also because it was so hard to drag myself out of bed knowing full well that I didn't have the emotional fortitude to focus on work, or even be around people at all. It was far easier when I could just stay home, zone out in front of the TV, or cry myself to sleep multiple times a day and just pretend the rest of the world had stopped to wait for me.

Each time I left the apartment was a brutal reminder that everyone, and everything, would continue to keep on moving whether I was ready or not. I hated the fact that each sunrise meant I was moving farther and farther away from the last time I saw my brother. The evenings weren't quite as bad, because I was just exhausted from fighting through my sadness all day. And by the time I'd been home from work for an hour, I was typically three glasses of wine and two sleeping pills into my evening regimen. By that time I would just wait for my body to relax into the chemically-induced sleep that was sure to come.

I've noticed that now there isn't really a time of day that's harder than others; the grief can creep up on me quickly at any time and it's usually triggered by something that reminds me of Brian. It could be seeing a car that looks just like his, hearing a song that he loved, or driving past a restaurant he loved. Honestly, having spent thirty-five years of my life with him, there isn't much out there that doesn't remind me of him. I see and hear reminders everywhere. But there isn't a single day that passes when he isn't on my mind.

*

MARCELLA MALONE
Marcella's 20-year-old brother
Michael died by suicide in 2014

The hardest time of day for me since Michael's loss has definitely been night. It's the time of day when my mind wonders and brings out the questions. Why? What if? What could have been? I begin to remember all of our memories and the plans we had made as siblings for our future and wonder how my life is going to be different without him in them.

It's too quiet after everyone is in bed, and it brings up a lot of sadness for me. Some nights are better than others, but in the last year and a half it hasn't gotten much easier for me. The hardest part is when I let my mind wander too much prior to falling asleep, because then the nightmares I had in the beginning come back. I see Michael with the shotgun under his chin. I see the tears in his eyes as he pulls the trigger. I see the gore of what happens as the bullet hits him and his lifeless body remains. At this point I wake up in panic and tears. I get my son out of his crib and bring him to my bed and just watch as he sleeps, remembering I have something to live for. Luckily, these occurrences have decreased from every time I shut my eyes to once every couple of weeks. The nights have gotten easier, but the struggle is still very much there.

*

BROOKE NINNI MATTHEWS
Brooke's 31-year-old brother Timothy
died by homicide in 2012

I really struggle with nighttime, especially when I'm in bed trying to fall asleep. It seems that no matter how hard I try, that morning replays in my mind all the time. I think about how the whole murder took place that morning.

*

NICKI NOBLE
Nicki's 43-year-old brother Don
died from a heart attack in 2004

This is hard to say because there can be anytime that I just think of my sweet brother and get sad. I can't say that there is any particular time of day that it hits me harder.

*

BRIDGET PARK
Bridget's brother Austin died
by suicide in 2008 at age 14

The hardest time of day for me is when I am sitting in class or I am not completely occupied doing something. Then I then think about my brother's suicide. I visualize his dead body on the floor next to the gun he had stuck into his mouth. I am forever haunted by this image, because no matter how hard I try to forget it, it pops into my head at the most random times. When this happens, I feel a surge of heat rushing through my body and tears in my eyes. Then I try to think about something happy, or happy memories of my brother. It saddens me that the way I think and remember my brother is this image, so I try to condition my brain to replace it with a better memory and image of him.

*

MARYELLEN ROACH
MaryEllen's 41-year-old sister Suzette
died in a car accident in 2012

At first, every single second was the hardest time of day. Sometimes late evenings on Wednesdays were harder, because the last time I saw Suzette was the Wednesday night before the accident, when she was getting ready and then leaving for work. Other times, Thursday evenings were harder because the accident happened around 8:30 p.m. on a Thursday.

As a general statement, I would have to say that nighttime after 9 p.m. is the most difficult. It seems that when everything outside my door has calmed down and others are sleeping, that's when my mind starts to go into overdrive. The sadness and despair creep in, the memories start playing in my head like a home movie, and sometimes it's completely overwhelming.

*

MICHAEL SMITH
Michael's 39-year-old brother Patrick
was killed by an impaired driver in 2007

Waking up was hardest. Patrick was three hours ahead of me and he would call on his work break at 10, which was 7 a.m. for me. Pat was the first person I talked to each day, and now that doesn't happen anymore. Has it changed? Not really. I have different routines, but I think about it every morning.

*

DAWN WOINOVICK
Dawn's 52-year-old brother
Todd died from cancer in 2013

Afternoon because a lot of the times we spent together were during the day. There was this big dark empty space. Actually there wasn't just a single specific time, we would touch base whenever. If I needed something fixed or had a question, or had some news I wanted to share, those were a lot of times. My youngest daughter was close to her Uncle Todd so when we get together we see something or hear something and almost in unison we say, "Uncle

Todd would love that," or, "Uncle Todd would say something about that."

But for the hardest days, and there are still a lot of them like birthdays, anniversary of his death, even just "I love you" days, I go to his grave with a helium balloon. I write him a message telling him I love and miss him, and send it straight to heaven. So I guess the hardest time of the day was October 20, 2013, the day Todd walked the stairs to heaven.

*

CHAPTER FIFTEEN

OUR FEAR

The oldest and strongest emotion of mankind is fear, and the oldest and strongest kind of fear is fear of the unknown. -H. P. LOVECRAFT

Fear can cut like a knife and immobilize us like a straitjacket. It whispers to us that our lives will never be the same, our misfortunes will manifest themselves again, and that we are helpless. How do we control our fear, so it doesn't control us?

*

EMILY BAIRD-LEVINE
Emily's 43-year-old brother Don
died from a heart attack in 2004

The loss of my brother brings up fear of the next loss. It also dredges up past losses. I so easily find myself allowing past grief and loss to come back to me. I fear the feelings that overwhelm me and take over. I am afraid that next time it happens, I won't be able to handle and endure it. The passing of time since Don's death hasn't changed this fear. It remains what it is. I accept that.

*

CHRISTINE BASTONE
Christine's 38-year-old sister
Liz died by suicide in 2012

I am most afraid of losing a family member to death...and of course I don't just mean my parents and my sister, but also my husband and my kids. Both the family I grew up with, and the family I live with now. My second worst fear is that my sister will be forgotten. I now consider it one of my "jobs" as her big sister to make sure that she isn't ever forgotten. Neither one of those fears are likely to change any time soon.

*

SHANNON BOOS
Shannon's 21-year-old brother Kevin
was killed by two drunk drivers in 2015

I am most afraid of losing someone else. I've lost people before Kevin, but it was never a loss like this. I've lost grandparents who were sick, and distant relatives whom I was never really close to. But a loss like this is something that I can't even compare to anything else.

I remember when two girls from my high school were killed by a drunk driver. It was about two years before Kevin was killed. At the time, I knew one of the girls' brothers, not well, but I knew him. I remember seeing him a few months later and staring at him in disbelief that he was surviving after losing a sibling that traumatically. I couldn't even imagine losing one of my brothers. Two years later, I went through the exact same thing. And now I can imagine it.

Sometimes I get into deep thought about death. I can actually picture myself losing other people, other loved ones. How would I handle it if my dad died? My mom? My other brother? It's not an "I can't imagine" thought anymore. I can imagine. I can feel it deep in my heart and in my soul. I have felt a pain I thought I would never feel, and I never want to feel it again.

I understand that death is inevitable. Everyone dies, it's natural. But the way my brother died was not natural in any sense of the word. I don't want to lose anyone like that ever again that quickly. Here one minute, and gone the next. No time for goodbyes or "I love you." Just gone.

I still jump when my phone rings. I get horrible flashbacks of the phone call saying that my brother had been in a car crash. It isn't so scary when it is in the middle of the day, or when it is my mom who calls me just about every day. It is when it is a person who doesn't call me very often calls at a strange hour. When that happens I already have it all running through my head. "Who died? What happened? Is everyone okay?" And it always just ends up being a regular, ordinary phone call. Except my heart is beating ten times its normal speed.

I hope that all my loved ones die peacefully many years from now, and that I never go through something like this again. Because this is something I will never recover from.

*

LISA FORESTBIRD
Lisa's 40-year-old brother Rob died
from a pontine hemorrhage in 2006

It's less a fear than a sadness. Sad I don't have Rob and we won't grow old together. I fear once my parents leave me that it will really feel like I am alone, at least as far as my nuclear family goes. So I suppose losing my mom and dad.

*

BONNIE FORSHEY
Bonnie's 54-year-old sister Eunice
died from bladder cancer in 2010

I do fear bladder cancer, because it killed her. Otherwise I have had so many losses, that I no longer fear anything.

*

LAURA HABEDANK
Laura's brother Brian died
by suicide in 2010 at age 35

I'm realizing that I'm afraid of spending my golden years alone. I'm divorced, live by myself, and have no children. I always figured that years from now, after my parents had passed on, that Brian and I would have each other. Now that he's gone I fear spending my golden years with absolutely zero family to speak of. I guess it doesn't scare me so much as it just makes me sad.

I have shared this with only a few people until now, but there was a brief period shortly after Brian died when I was considering trying to have a baby with my ex-husband. Those feelings didn't last long, fortunately, because it would have been a terrible idea. I've never had the urge to have children at any point in my life, and the fears of dying alone and of my family's gene pool dying with me were terrible reasons to have reconsidered that, even briefly. But my deepest fear, by far, is the fear of my own depression. I've struggled with it for as far back as I can remember. I have so many memories of feeling suicidal throughout my entire life, dating back to my early childhood. For the most part I have it under control now, but I'm always afraid of when the next episode is going to hit, because they are absolutely unbearable. I hate the feeling of utter hopelessness and worthlessness that come along with the episodes, and the amount of effort it takes to just get through each day. It's so exhausting—week after week after week. Sometimes the idea of having to go back to the doctor, re-evaluate my prescriptions and adjust the dosage, or the dreaded change of medication altogether, is just so overwhelming. It's hard to muster up the energy to go through all of that—the tapering off of one medication, the ramping up of a new one, and praying the side effects won't be worse than the depression itself and that it will actually work; because if it doesn't, you start the whole difficult process back over again.

*

MARCELLA MALONE
Marcella's 20-year-old brother
Michael died by suicide in 2014

Since the loss of Michael, I am most afraid of not doing my best to prevent any of my loved ones, or simply those I meet each day, from feeling so helpless that they make the same decision he did. I make sure I am there when anyone needs me, and I am extra conscious of the necessity of ending each conversation with an "I love you," or some other positive departure. The little things are what I am most afraid of missing out on.

My outlook on life has definitely changed. This comes out the most when it comes to my parenting. My son just celebrated his first birthday, but my biggest fear is going through the pain my parents live with each day. It's unimaginable and unbearable.

*

BROOKE NINNI MATTHEWS
Brooke's 31-year-old brother Timothy
died by homicide in 2012

I worry most about losing someone I love horrifically again. I also worry about what this world is coming to, it seems others just don't care about human life anymore. Nobody wants to talk and work things out anymore, they're just quick to pull out a weapon of choice.

*

NICKI NOBLE
Nicki's 43-year-old brother Don
died from a heart attack in 2004

Losing another loved one.

*

BRIDGET PARK
Bridget's brother Austin died
by suicide in 2008 at age 14

I am afraid that one day my children will ask if I have any siblings and how my brother died. I remember when my mother first told me that her brother had died, and it was very confusing to me. She told me that he got sick and died, but she was just protecting me from the fact that he died by suicide. I am deathly afraid for this day. If and when it comes, not only does it pain me, but I can relate to my children's curiosity and confusion on the subject. It made me sad as a child to have missed out on having an uncle and possibly having cousins.

I would never tell my children the truth of my brother's death if they asked me when they were still too young to understand it. I would lie to them as my mother did to me, for their own protection. I do not think it is wrong at all to do so, because it is for their own protection.

*

MARYELLEN ROACH
MaryEllen's 41-year-old sister Suzette
died in a car accident in 2012

In general I try not to live in fear. But with grief, unfortunately, comes a huge amount of fear, at least for me. Pinpointing what I'm most afraid of is very difficult. I'm scared that I will forget things about Suzette, like how she smelled, how brushing and fixing her hair felt, what her voice sounded like and about things we did together and talked about. I'm afraid that I will never be able to look at photos of her again without completely breaking down. I could look at Suzette's pictures for a couple of months after her move to heaven, but for some reason that changed and it has been completely overwhelming for me since. I have pictures of her around my house, I just don't stop and really look at them. If I do really look at photos of her, it takes me right back to the extremely deep, dark hole of grief that feels completely hopeless and makes me wonder how I can keep breathing. I'm terrified that something will happen to the cards and other things Suzette made for me. The things she made and the photos I have are truly priceless and of course irreplaceable. I have all there is ever going to be.

About a month before the accident, my parents, Suzette, Lillian, Vivian, and I all took a vacation to Florida. Suzette, the girls and I went to Disney World for the first two days of vacation. My parents didn't want to go to Disney World and instead enjoyed time around the hotel and exploring the area, which meant it was just the four of us making memories at Disney. I'm afraid that I will forget things we did and it's so scary because I'm the only one left to remember. Another huge fear I have is losing my parents which would mean more life changes than I can even imagine. I know it will happen eventually because life ends, but it terrifies me. I never used to think about how nice it is to have people who have always known me, who remember things I did when I was a child or remember things that happened during my childhood even if it didn't involve me. Since Suzette was seven years older and is now gone, my parents are the only two who have those memories. I just cannot imagine life without them, nor do I want to.

*

MICHAEL SMITH
Michael's 39-year-old brother Patrick
was killed by an impaired driver in 2007

I realized after my brother was killed that I was not immortal. Believe it or not, I became afraid to fly, and of the takeoff especially. I would imagine all kinds of terrible things that could happen to the plane; the noises from taking off literally freaked me out and I had to take pills from a nurse neighbor so I could calm down and not be very uncomfortable. Has it improved? A little, but now I am much more cautious than I ever was.

*

DAWN WOINOVICK
Dawn's 52-year-old brother
Todd died from cancer in 2013

Since Todd died of cancer, that of course would be something on my heart. But losing my folks actually become my biggest fear, because what I believed to be the real world, parents die and brother and sisters go through that together, well that ship sailed. Now if I lost my folks I would be all alone in the world. My brother and I both were divorced. I have three children but a relationship with only one. So as for another adult to grow through such a grief with, well I guess that's why it's what I'm most afraid of.

CHAPTER SIXTEEN

OUR COMFORT

Life is made up not of great sacrifices or duties, but of little things, in which smiles and kindness, and small obligations given habitually, preserve the heart and secure comfort. -HUMPHRY DAVY

Transition sometimes feels as if we have embarked on a foreign journey with no companion, compass, or light. Rather than fill our bag with necessities, we often seek to fill it with emotional items that bring us comfort as we find our way through the eye of the storm. What items or rituals bring you the most comfort?

*

EMILY BAIRD-LEVINE
Emily's 43-year-old brother Don
died from a heart attack in 2004

Probably the most comfort comes from remembering and sharing good things about Don and talking to others who understand this loss and are willing to share and listen. My sister is a huge comfort. Another great comfort is to donate in Don's memory to his college alma mater, Pomona College. Those were good years for him when he was surrounded by friends who remained his friends until his passing.

I also embrace the Jewish tradition of doing good deeds in Don's memory. According to Judaism, doing good deeds in a loved one's merit elevates their soul. This is a comfort.

*

CHRISTINE BASTONE
Christine's 38-year-old sister
Liz died by suicide in 2012

Anything that makes me feel connected to my sister. This could mean eating something that she liked, seeing the sign from her of "210," feeling her presence, hearing her voice inside my head...anything and everything that makes me feel connected to her. A close second is when anyone mentions her name, or otherwise remembers or honors her. And by "remember," I don't just mean the people who actually knew Liz while she was alive. There are a lot of people in my online support groups who have asked me about her, or made a comment to me about her, or who have attended my Facebook event that I have every year for Liz...who have never met her. But when they do those kinds of things that I just mentioned, it still greatly comforts me.

*

SHANNON BOOS
Shannon's 21-year-old brother Kevin
was killed by two drunk drivers in 2015

The thing that brings me the most comfort is signs from Kevin. I notice them all the time, in the smallest of things. I don't know if I believe in God, but I do believe there is some sort of afterlife or heaven. I know Kevin has to be somewhere. An amazing person with a beautiful soul doesn't just disappear. He has to be somewhere. And wherever he is, I know he is trying hard to communicate with me and let me know that he is okay.

I have dreams of him telling me he is okay. I have dreams of him hugging me. I see his face in strangers that look so much like him it makes me look twice. I see butterflies and birds that fly right in front of my face and snap me out of sad, grieving thoughts.

The first time I visited Kevin's grave by myself I just sat there. I was crying, and talking, not even sure if he could hear me. I felt like I was wasting my time, so between tears I said out loud, "Kevin, if you're here and you can hear me, please, *please*, just give me some sort of sign."

A butterfly came. And it didn't just flutter by. It flew in circles around my head for about fifteen seconds while I cried and laughed and smiled and said "Hi, Kevin!" loudly.

THAT brings me comfort. That I can still feel his love and our bond even though I can't see him.

*

LISA FORESTBIRD
Lisa's 40-year-old brother Rob died
from a pontine hemorrhage in 2006

Living life to the fullest brings me comfort, because when I do, my brother is with me. That is really all I can do; try to make the most of my life and not take it for granted. I like to think I am living for two, although sometimes that can feel a bit exhausting.

*

BONNIE FORSHEY
Bonnie's 54-year-old sister Eunice
died from bladder cancer in 2010

I find comfort in my memories and photographs. I also have comfort when I look at the pictures that my sister's children post online. I find comfort looking at their faces. I see my sister in their eyes and smiles. I have a few items that belonged to my sister, they gave her joy, and they remind me of her. I also love my photographs of her, they mean the world to me.

*

LAURA HABEDANK
Laura's brother Brian died
by suicide in 2010 at age 35

For me, it is so comforting to know that Brian isn't suffering anymore. Depression is such a cruel and unforgiving illness. I found out only five months before Brian took his own life that he had attempted suicide twice before, once when we were roommates in our mid-twenties. I had no idea that he and I were both experiencing periods of such darkness at the same time, in rooms ten feet from each other. We lived together, ate together, went to movies together yet neither of us wanted to burden the other with the heaviness we were feeling. As much as I hate to admit this, there was a small part of me that was relieved when he died, because I'd spent the previous months in agony wondering if he was okay and panicking each time he didn't answer his phone. I was relieved that he was now free of the darkness that had been weighing him down his entire life.

It also brings me so much comfort to talk about Brian and reminisce over photographs and emails and mementoes. In the beginning I didn't do much of it, because it was still too hard and the panic attacks were never far behind; I had to know my limits and know when I was in a good place to sit down with those things and just have a good cry. Nowadays I find myself smiling more when going through my pictures of him, and I feel less agony and a little more peace because I think I've done a good job of grieving exactly as I needed to—I never forced myself to ignore the feelings that came up; I felt them, processed them and let them go. After five years of that, I'm in a place where there are more smiles than tears when I talk about him.

I've received a great deal of comfort from meeting other survivors, particularly other sibling survivors. Losing someone to suicide complicates the grieving process, I believe. Aside from the intense pain and sadness, there are the added feelings of guilt, shame, anger, shock, abandonment, and even relief, as I mentioned earlier. It can be such an alienating experience, because very few people know what to say, so they end up either saying the wrong things or ignoring the bereaved altogether. I met some wonderful friends, fellow sister survivors, at a suicide loss support group, and have met some amazing people through my occasional volunteer efforts regarding suicide awareness and prevention. I was also fortunate enough to be included in a documentary about sibling suicide produced by Caley Cook, entitled *Four Sisters*. The other three sisters also live here in Austin, Texas, and have become my friends. We don't often see each other, but it's been wonderful to be able to get together and know that we all understand one another in a way that others don't. It was difficult to talk about and even more difficult to see it on film two years later, but there was also some incredible healing that came to me because of it, and it felt good to be in a position to help other people going through the same thing.

A few days after Brian died, a family friend gave us a poem about pennies being little reminders that our loved one is letting us know they are around. I didn't think too much of the poem at first, but when we were going through Brian's things it came to mean so much more. When cleaning out his bedroom, the last thing I emptied was his clothes hamper. After I removed the clothes, I carried all the bags I'd collected out into the living room, leaving the hamper where I had found it. About half an hour later my mom went back in there to get the hamper from his room, and she came out with a such look on her face, a look of awe, hope, and pain all at the same time. She stretched out her hand and showed me something she found when she lifted the hamper from its place. It was a single penny. Thinking back to the poem about the pennies, I felt myself choking up. But it got better. I turned the penny over to see that it was dated 1975, the year Brian was born. I immediately burst into tears, and it made my heart smile to think that Brian sent that penny to let us know he was there. I have been collecting all the pennies I find since he passed. I tend to find them in the strangest places and at moments just when I need them most.

*

MARCELLA MALONE
Marcella's 20-year-old brother
Michael died by suicide in 2014

I find the most comfort in the simple things that remind me of Michael. My favorite thing is his Red Wings windbreaker. He got it at a game we went to a year prior to his death. It's one of my many fond memories with him. If I'm having a particularly rough day, I'll put it on to remind myself that I have the best angel looking out for me, making sure I will make it through the challenges life throws my way. Wearing it is like getting a hug from Michael, reminding me he is still there whether I see him or not.

*

BROOKE NINNI MATTHEWS
Brooke's 31-year-old brother Timothy
died by homicide in 2012

Wearing my brother's shirts or socks, I also love wrapping

myself in the memory quilt I made out of his clothes. It also brings me comfort to share stories and memories about him, and share pictures of him. I also find comfort knowing that his spirit lives on and if I make myself aware of that, I'll see the signs he sends me.

*

NICKI NOBLE
Nicki's 43-year-old brother Don
died from a heart attack in 2004

What brings me comfort is talking about my sweet brother, looking at photos of him and quoting some of his funny sayings.

*

MARYELLEN ROACH
MaryEllen's 41-year-old sister Suzette
died in a car accident in 2012

The biggest comfort I have is definitely knowing that Suzette, Lillian, and Vivian are in heaven and they are in my future. As strange as it may seem to some and, although I miss all three of them beyond words, I find it very comforting that Suzette and the girls aren't here and instead are in a place that's full of love and free from the negative things we have on earth. I no longer have to worry about something happening to them like cancer or another illness. Suzette is no longer stressed out and exhausted from work, there's no fear or danger where they are now. The "worst" has already happened, they died a physical death, but I'm thankful they were gone instantly and didn't suffer. There are much worse ways they could have left this earth.

It is also comforting to know that Suzette, Lillian, and Vivian will be among other loved ones who will greet me when my time on earth is finally done. We will all be reunited and never have to leave each other again.

*

MICHAEL SMITH
Michael's 39-year-old brother Patrick
was killed by an impaired driver in 2007

Nothing brings me comfort. The memory is always there. Sure, there are distractions, but comfort? Nothing.

*

DAWN WOINOVICK
Dawn's 52-year-old brother
Todd died from cancer in 2013

My trust in God. Some people reading this might, at this point, be ready to throw this book across the room. But I assure you that I'm not bible banging here. When you've lost something so dear to you as a very special person in your life, running to the fridge for a cold beer or a pint of ice cream just won't do the job. Let me save you a few steps. Grief is a different kind of emotion. It is not one that will just go away. It will steal everything including your soul unless you confront it head on. Stand face to face, get right up close, look into you mirror and say, "You're going down, grief! I'm fighting back."

OK, now you're ready. Give yourself permission to cry, be angry, hit something but not someone, something. Yell, scream, get pissed. The person who just left you isn't coming back, so tell them how you feel, it's okay. TELL THEM really, right now, they still can hear. This is the only true way to getting back your comfort. I'll pray for you, and if you need help, search me out through this program, but only if you are serious about finding comfort through grief.

*

CHAPTER SEVENTEEN

OUR SILVER LINING

Even a small star shines in darkness.
-FINNISH PROVERB

In the earliest days following loss, the thought that anything good can come from our experience is beyond comprehension. Yet some say there are blessings in everything. Have you discovered a silver lining in your loss?

*

EMILY BAIRD-LEVINE
Emily's 43-year-old brother Don
died from a heart attack in 2004

The most immediate silver lining that I identified soon after losing my brother is that I got to know his fiancée, Kitty, much better. Only after Don's passing did I learn of the plans that he and Kitty had. They planned to get married and Don was going to finance Kitty's medical school education. In addition, she shared many details of travels and adventures that they experienced together, along with future plans that they had made. I feel like only after Don died did Kitty really feel like family, like my sister-in-law. To this day, having this relationship with Kitty is a blessing.

*

CHRISTINE BASTONE
Christine's 38-year-old sister
Liz died by suicide in 2012

I now know that the most important part of a person is his or hers presence. And that the outward appearances and circumstances of any loved one's life, myself included, pale in comparison to that.

*

SHANNON BOOS
Shannon's 21-year-old brother Kevin
was killed by two drunk drivers in 2015

I don't believe there was a purpose for Kevin dying, or that it "happened for a reason" like so many people love to tell me. I have been trying to be more positive in life, and although most of the time it is unbearable just thinking about how he is gone, I try and make something out of it.

My family and I started this project we call Live Like Kevin. Kevin was known for his random acts of kindness. After he died, we had random people come up to us and just start talking about Kevin. The security guard of our neighborhood actually came up to us and said that Kevin was the only one in the whole neighborhood who talked to him. He said Kevin would even bring him donuts and chat with him for a while. The mail carrier said Kevin would always come up to her and strike up a conversation and ask how her day was going. It was always so shocking to her, but she told us she would never forget it, because it always made her day.

The project Live Like Kevin is dedicated to random acts of kindness. I had business cards made that are used to entice people to pay it forward. For example, I'll pay for the person's food who is in line behind me, and then give them one of the cards. Sometimes I'll tell Kevin's story, sometimes I won't. But on the card is his picture and a link to our Facebook page, and I ask people to please perform a random act of kindness for someone else and ask them to pass on Kevin's card.

I love making people happy in Kevin's honor. It makes me feel so much better, and this is when I feel closest to him. Although I would give all of it up just to have him back, I know it makes him happy to see us making something from his absence.

That is my silver lining—that his memory is still alive, and Kevin is still making people happy, even when he's not here.

*

LISA FORESTBIRD
Lisa's 40-year-old brother Rob died
from a pontine hemorrhage in 2006

I can relate to others suffering from loss and that exact bond has created and rekindled friendships. I now take very little for granted. When people live to a ripe-old age, I now find that to be a miracle. I have discovered life is fragile. I can no longer rely on Rob for worldly issues. This has forced me to become more self-reliant on myself and others too, in a positive way. I have gotten closer to my parents and can more frankly speak of our own immortality.

*

BONNIE FORSHEY
Bonnie's 54-year-old sister Eunice
died from bladder cancer in 2010

I don't see any silver lining in the loss of my sister. She suffered terribly, and left behind three children. They lost their mother, their home, and everything they ever had. They all went in different

185

directions, to start over. I lost my sister, and she had been in my life since birth. All of our lives have drastically changed, and there is a huge void left.

*

LAURA HABEDANK
Laura's brother Brian died
by suicide in 2010 at age 35

It could be the suicide loss, and it could just be my getting older and more mature, or a combination of both, but I've grown stronger. I can handle more than I ever dreamed possible. I am getting better at sticking up for myself more, and I find that I'm more likely to rid myself of relationships that are harmful to me or don't serve me well. Throughout a number of difficult losses in my life since Brian died, I've reminded myself that I will get through it. If I can manage to survive losing Brian like I did, I can surely overcome other losses too.

I've become more open with others about my own struggle with depression, self-injury, and suicidality. I want to increase awareness for the good of all who suffer from it, but also to help others who have lost someone close to them to suicide. I think I have a unique perspective to offer. Not only have I had someone close to me die by suicide, but I've also been seconds away from taking my own life on multiple occasions. I can understand the mindset behind someone making that choice for himself, as well as the thought process of someone trying to cope with the aftermath of that choice.

This grief journey has also made me more caring toward others. I think anyone who has suffered naturally develops a more compassionate nature, because he knows pain and doesn't wish to see anyone suffer as he has. There are some seemingly benign changes of which I'm aware, like how I relate to others. If I am stuck behind someone at a stoplight who is not moving when the light turns green, my initial reaction is to honk and get him moving again. But then I recall the days and weeks and months following Brian's death when I drove around in a complete daze and would often just space out at a light until I was startled out of my tearful moment of remembrance by the honk of the car behind me. If someone is rude or abrasive toward me, my knee-jerk reaction is to be upset or snap back. But if I take another moment to think about it, I remember how early on I was in a constant state of "fight or flight," and with my emotions so close to the surface I could blurt out things I didn't mean, because I was acting out of pain. I've been trying to remain mindful of the fact that each person is fighting his own kind of battle and to be respectful of that. It's not always easy to do, but I try to be aware of that as much as possible.

Finally, I think this process has helped me become less anxious. Anxiety is still an issue for me, but not to the degree that it used to be. I guess when compared to the death of my brother few things really compare in their importance, and I'm getting better at not obsessing over things that just don't matter. I'm learning how to "pick my battles" within my relationships and try to really focus on the larger issues that are most important to me.

*

MARCELLA MALONE
Marcella's 20-year-old brother
Michael died by suicide in 2014

April 14, 2014, thus far the worst day of my life, the day I had to face the reality that my brother chose to leave this earth and his family behind, has somehow amazingly but slowly shown a silver lining in my life. Don't get me wrong, each day is a struggle and still brings me pain, but my brother's loss has also taught me the value of each day. I had always taken each day for granted, as well as Michael's presence in all the events of my future. After his loss I struggled with the fact that I didn't see it coming and couldn't stop it. I went to my comfort of research and read everything I could find on suicide and sibling loss. I discovered that he was in the highest risk group as a young male. Those seen as the strongest frequently lose their battle with their inside demons. This hit me hard. I began looking at each day as an opportunity to bring a smile to someone's face. I began making time for family and friends. I put in a stronger effort to get along with the other half of my son's family. These people and things are no longer taken for granted. No matter how angry I may be, I do my best to end everything with "I love you." It may not seem like much, but this new outlook on life has made a major impact on my life and greatly assisted in my grief journey.

*

BROOKE NINNI MATTHEWS
Brooke's 31-year-old brother Timothy
died by homicide in 2012

The horrific loss of my only brother has made me realize that my daughter feels comfortable coming and talking to me with anything on her mind, or any problem she may have. It took me a year to see that. When she wanted to go to heaven with my brother, it was then she really opened up to me, and is now always open about all things. It also made me see that my son, who is older than my daughter, got short-sighted with many things, just as I saw my brother did growing up with four sisters. It was then when I realized that I wanted my son to be treated equal to his sister, and not be shorted just because she was the girl, like my brother had because of his four sisters.

*

MICHAEL SMITH
Michael's 39-year-old brother Patrick
was killed by an impaired driver in 2007

I don't think there is or will be a silver lining regarding the horrible accident that killed my brother. There have been other families affected by impaired hypoglycemic drivers that I have been able to communicate with, and we all share these tragedies, but I wouldn't say I've yet found a silver lining. There was a terrible crash in San Jose caused by a Pacific Gas & Electric utility truck driver who accidentally double-dosed his insulin. His glucose level dropped so severely that he was impaired enough to plow his truck into a vehicle with two young college students inside. Mary Bernstein and her boyfriend were killed in the crash when their vehicle burst into flames. Her mother, Lisa Bernstein, forced many legal changes in the way California companies maintain driving records on their drivers, especially those with diabetes. So knowing her and what she was able to achieve was someone else's silver lining that I was able to appreciate.

*

DAWN WOINOVICK
Dawn's 52-year-old brother
Todd died from cancer in 2013

The silver lining is that tomorrow will be exactly two years that my brother Todd passed away, and I'm not the same sister he left behind. I am a woman who takes nothing for granted, not one breath, not one smile. I have always been a positive person but now I feel it and really live it. I see people and things so differently and I want to leave a good mark and make a difference. Until God calls me home, I'll keep watching and teaching about that silver lining because if you look hard enough there is one in everything.

SURVIVING LOSS OF A SIBLING

Not every day is beautiful,
but there is beauty in every day.

LYNDA CHELDELIN FELL

*

CHAPTER EIGHTEEN

OUR HOPE

Be like the birds, sing after every storm.
-BETH MENDE CONNY

Hope is the fuel that propels us forward, urges us to get out of bed each morning. It is the promise that tomorrow will be better than today. Each breath we take and each footprint we leave is a measure of hope. So is hope possible in the aftermath of loss? If so, where do we find it?

*

EMILY BAIRD-LEVINE
Emily's 43-year-old brother Don
died from a heart attack in 2004

To me hope is looking at each situation, each loss, each step backward as an opportunity to regroup, take stock, be grateful for what we do have in this life at the present. Hope is to learn how to shed light on the darkness, to make daily attempts at making this a better world, to carry on the legacies of the loved ones whom we have lost, to be open to new opportunities and to learn from the mistakes we have made. Hope is going forward and making every moment of every day count.

*

CHRISTINE BASTONE
Christine's 38-year-old sister
Liz died by suicide in 2012

Hope is when you believe that somehow, someway, things will get better some day. Hope is also the knowledge that one day can change everything. It can be for the worse, or for the better. When I lost my sister, of course it was for the worse. I have hope that one day, things will change for the better. I feel that hope is also wanting to see how everything turns out. It is living out the saying, "Where there is life, there is hope." And not wanting to exit, so to speak, right before things get better!

*

SHANNON BOOS
Shannon's 21-year-old brother Kevin
was killed by two drunk drivers in 2015

I believe that hope is the feeling you get when you know that no matter how horrible things are now, it will get better.

Although life without Kevin is so dark, and even unbearable at times, I hold on to hope that I will see him again. Wherever he is, I will be there one day, and he will be waiting. He will have that big, goofy grin on his face, and will give me the huge hug that I've needed for so long.

"Shannonnnnnnnn! I missed you!" He'll look at me as if it has been only a day or two, like we are just meeting up for coffee. I'll collapse in his arms with happiness, unable to stand because I am so overwhelmed with relief. I'm finally with my best friend again.

Hope for me is that somewhere out there is a world where Kevin Boos exists. Kevin Boos still has his huge smile, and that one dimple on his cheek. He is surrounded by mashed potatoes, Pop Tarts, music, and all of our loved ones. He is waiting for me, and I will be there with him.

Some day. I hope.

*

LISA FORESTBIRD
Lisa's 40-year-old brother Rob died
from a pontine hemorrhage in 2006

Well, I hope I stay healthy and can live a long life and have rich and rewarding relationships. My hope is to live a full life and make the most of my gifts and experiences, for life is too short to squander anything.

*

BONNIE FORSHEY
Bonnie's 54-year-old sister Eunice
died from bladder cancer in 2010

I don't think I can honestly answer this question, I lost so much hope when my sister passed away. I just want her children to be happy again and have good lives. They lost everything, and at such young ages. She was a single mother, and was all that they had.

*

LAURA HABEDANK
Laura's brother Brian died
by suicide in 2010 at age 35

I think this is the most difficult of all of these questions for me. I mean, I know what the textbook definition of "hope" is, but truthfully I just haven't felt a whole lot of it since Brian took his life. I've been capable of feeling happiness and joy and enjoyment, and have been able to laugh again, but so far "hope" has eluded me. I keep telling myself that the best I can do is to keep moving forward and maybe someday a little hope will come back to my life. I guess you could say that I'm "hopeful that one day I'll have hope again." In the words of Forrest Gump, "That's all I have to say about that."

*

BROOKE NINNI MATTHEWS
Brooke's 31-year-old brother Timothy
died by homicide in 2012

I've learned that hope means something so much different than what it did before my brother's murder. I live my life so much different than I did four years ago. I now am not afraid to let others know the true me. I stick to my beliefs, I try to understand others and not to judge, and don't pretend to be someone I'm not just because society wants me or tells me to be that way. I am who I am. I think just by being yourself and living with peace and love in your heart, the world will someday be a much better place.

*

MICHAEL SMITH
Michael's 39-year-old brother Patrick
was killed by an impaired driver in 2007

This is going to sound terrible, but I am waiting for an impaired diabetic to cause an accident involving someone famous or important. It is the only way I can see the public and especially state officials realizing that this is a very dangerous and largely ignored public problem, and that there needs to be legislation to watch over people who are at risk of getting behind the wheel with low blood sugar and to take away the driver's license of those who have a track record of causing accidents in this manner.

The man who killed my brother never even received a traffic ticket for running a red light. His license was suspended at my urging. However, through his doctor, the State of Connecticut allowed him to reinstate it three months later. Nothing happened to this man. My family, however, was forever changed, and my brother suffered a horrible death. He wasn't killed instantly; eyewitnesses I spoke to said he was breathing and moaning for several minutes afterward.

*

DAWN WOINOVICK
Dawn's 52-year-old brother
Todd died from cancer in 2013

Hope is always believing what you cannot see, even when it doesn't make sense. Know in your heart what you know. Even if you feel like God isn't faithful, know that he is. If you don't feel like God is loving you right now, know that he does. When it feels like he has forgotten us and what we are going through, know that he is here. Don't feel like God still has a plan for you, know he does. Hope to me is faith, feeling sometimes you just have to know what you know.

Let it all be still, and just know.

*

Your parents leave you too soon and
your kids and spouse come along late,
but your siblings know you when you are
in your most inchoate form.

JEFFREY KLUGER

*

CHAPTER NINETEEN

OUR JOURNEY

Be soft. Do not let the world make you hard. Do not let the pain make you hate. Do not let bitterness steal your sweetness. -KURT VONNEGUT

Every journey through loss is as unique as one's fingerprint, for we experience different beliefs, different desires, different needs, different tolerances, and often we walk different roads. Though we may not see anyone else on the path, we are never truly alone for more walk behind, beside, and in front of us. In this chapter lies the answers to the final question posed: What would you like the world to know about your grief journey?

*

EMILY BAIRD-LEVINE
Emily's 43-year-old brother Don
died from a heart attack in 2004

My grief journey has been a rollercoaster of ups and downs. It has definitely forced me to become stronger and more resilient. It has reminded me to keep going forward, to be grateful, and to be compassionate for others who also grieve. All the while, I try to keep in the forefront that everyone's journey is their own and there are no time limits on grief. It is a long-term process that doesn't go away, but merely morphs over time. Sometimes, it feels like it goes back to the moment when Don took his last breath, and sometimes it feels like the almost eleven years since he died. I never know when a memory, good or bad, will bring streams of tears or bursts of laughter thinking of my wonderful and silly brother.

*

CHRISTINE BASTONE
Christine's 38-year-old sister
Liz died by suicide in 2012

What I would like the world to know is that losing a sibling is a huge loss. My sister was a part of who I am. I lost a piece of myself. I also lost a piece of my past, a piece of our history of growing up together is gone now. I lost a piece of my present...our relationship when we became adults, the one we had when she died. And I lost a piece of my future, we were supposed to grow old together.

Many siblings feel like it is one of their jobs to protect each other. So then when a sibling dies, we have obviously failed at that job somewhere. I don't think that I quite realized that I felt this way until after Liz died. And even though my head tells me that there's no way I could have known, and that there is likely nothing that I could have done, my heart feels like I completely failed at my "job" of protecting my youngest sister. I expect my heart to always feel that way. I do not expect that to change and that's okay.

Us siblings feel very deeply for the pain of our parents, and actually for any parent who has lost a child, but most of all for our own. We wish we could take that pain away, but we also suffered a huge loss, and people need to remember that. Because sometimes that huge loss is minimized, or even dismissed.

My sister was a parallel traveler in my life, and I lost that traveler. That loss was very shocking. I fully expected her to always be there. And it didn't matter whether or not I had tons of contact with her, or whether or not the relationship was difficult. She's still my sister; that fact trumps all of that. That fact trumps everything!

Liz lived in Ohio; I live in Florida. So for the last seventeen years of her life we didn't see each other all that much. But even so, I still very keenly feel my loss.

Liz could be difficult. We weren't always close. And we didn't always have the best relationship. But I know that the sibling bond is much stronger and deeper than those things. Liz was always my "baby sister," no matter how old she got. And even now that she's no longer here in this physical world, she is still my "baby sister," and always will be.

*

SHANNON BOOS
Shannon's 21-year-old brother Kevin
was killed by two drunk drivers in 2015

I would like the world to know that losing Kevin is something that has affected me permanently, and has forever changed who I am as a person. This isn't a break up with a boyfriend, this isn't a broken bone — half my soul has left my body and I can't find it.

Whether a stranger, a friend, an acquaintance, or a family member is reading this, you should know that my grief isn't going to go away. I will never "get over it." I will never "move on."

I wrote a poem to express how my grief has impacted me, and how it affects me every day. I wrote it for myself, because writing has always been an outlet for me. I wrote it for others who are on this horrible journey with me, so they know they're not alone.

But mostly, I wrote it for those who tell me to move on, who think that this is something I could possibly get over. I wrote it for those who are so fortunate to never have felt pain like this, hoping that maybe they can try to understand.

Grief.

It may sound like a calm, somber feeling to you. It sounds soft. It sounds like smooth waves that strike you above your stomach when days are hard.

But grief is relentless and unforgiving.

It is still waters suddenly erupting into towering waves, knocking you to the ground, leaving your lungs full of water, not sure which way is up.

Grief is not sleeping soundly in the night, waking up with a few tears.

It is being torn to consciousness as Pain decides to dig its claws into your chest, daring you to try to breathe.

Grief is not a cloud that hangs over your head.

It is shackles tied to your ankles, your arms, your neck, your heart, confining you to the pain, when all you want to do is live free again.

Grief is not being surrounded by love and those you rely on holding you up.

It is turning around two weeks after he's gone, screaming into an empty room because there's no one there but yourself.

Grief is not a nightmare or two at night.

It is waking up with a pounding heart, thankful that this was all just a dream.

And then you realize that it wasn't just a dream.

This is real.

This is your new life.

And you have to live with it. Every. Single. Day.

Forever.

*

LISA FORESTBIRD
Lisa's 40-year-old brother Rob died
from a pontine hemorrhage in 2006

Rob passed away when he was transporting my Miata from the Midwest to Washington. He died in service to his sister. That created a special bond between us in his death. After our loss, I canceled my plans to relocate back to the West Coast. But then, just a year before the first anniversary of his passing, I got an exciting work opportunity in Washington. It was tempting to remain close to family, but my parents encouraged me to answer the call and embark on adventure, as had my brother both in his death and in his life. On the exact day of Rob's one year anniversary, I found myself surrounded by new faces, but in the familiar field of sunflowers I had encountered in the funeral home. I was on a journey in a new town, two thousand miles from home. I shed many tears but coped with my loss by living life, as full as I could.

Now, just a year shy of the tenth anniversary of Rob's passing, I have become a first time homeowner, and share the same street number as my parents, 1536. That was a sign I was home again. I know my parents will visit me a lot, but when the time comes, I will have peace knowing that I am exactly where I was meant to be.

*

BONNIE FORSHEY
Bonnie's 54-year-old sister Eunice
died from bladder cancer in 2010

I miss my sister, and have become very outspoken about bladder cancer. If my sister would have gone to the doctor earlier, she might still be alive today. Everyone should educate themselves about this disease.

*

LAURA HABEDANK
Laura's brother Brian died
by suicide in 2010 at age 35

If there is one thing I have learned, it is that there is no right or wrong way to grieve the loss of a loved one. Everyone is different, and what worked for me might not work for another. But sooner or later it does need to be dealt with.

I met a woman in the support group one evening who had lost someone close to her to suicide fifteen years earlier, but had never really allowed herself to grieve. She continued to push her feelings aside year after year, and eventually ended up hospitalized after having a nervous breakdown. She shared with us that she wished she had addressed her feelings years earlier.

There's also no set timeline for grief. The five stages of grief outlined by Elisabeth Kübler-Ross (denial, anger, bargaining, depression, and acceptance) can happen in any order, over and over and in combination with one another. I still find myself experiencing all of these stages, sometimes all in a single day, even five years later. I would want people to know that they should never force themselves, or anyone else, to move through grief any faster than what feels natural to them. There is never an appropriate time to tell someone, "You should be over it by now." The thing is, you don't ever get over it. You get through it and you get better at dealing with it, but you never get over it.

Having my brother choose to die left me feeling abandoned. I once asked him, knowing full well how deeply he was suffering, to promise me he wouldn't leave me. He told me he couldn't promise that. In hindsight, I regret asking that of him, because I know that had that same question been posed to me in the middle of a suicidal episode, I'd have been unable to promise it myself and would have resented anyone who asked it of me. But having been left behind like this, I've become increasingly afraid of abandonment and am working on that as it has certainly complicated some of my relationships and, sadly, even ended a few. I began going to support group meetings for suicide survivors only two weeks after Brian's death, not only because I really needed to talk openly about it, but also because all of my family and closest friends were 1,200 miles away. I desperately wanted to be around others who understood what I was going through. It was so important for me to find a support group specific to suicide, because I don't think I could have been nearly as open about my feelings about my brother's choice to end his own life while surrounded by people who were grieving the losses of people who fought valiant battles against cancer or were tragically killed in an accident. Death is death, but there was something so valuable to be shared among a group of survivors who had to deal with the fact that their loved ones chose to die. I'd also like people to know that a little support toward a grieving friend can go a long, long way. Even if you don't have the perfect words to say (because often those words just don't exist), just being there to listen is such an incredible gift.

*

MARCELLA MALONE
Marcella's 20-year-old brother
Michael died by suicide in 2014

My grief journey since Michael's death has definitely been an emotional rollercoaster. It's given me a new outlook on the world and helped me to better read the unspoken emotions of those around me. It's given me a new understanding on what I'm learning as I finish up my psychology degree, and, most importantly it has taught me a couple of important lessons.

The biggest thing I learned, and am still learning, is to not be afraid to talk about things. It is very unhealthy to hold your emotions in and appear to be something you're not. Talking about Michael's life helps me keep his memory alive and helps others to understand the depth of our loss. Talking about the impact of how he left this earth and how I'm coping with it has helped me to heal and shown me who is really there for me. Through conversation I have found a support that I could have never found myself through strangers and those close to me. Your journey should not be alone.

It also taught me the absolute value of those you love, and every day you are given together. It taught me not to hold grudges and to never miss an opportunity to tell someone how you feel about him or her. Life is way too short.

The biggest lesson it taught me was to never judge a book by its cover. Everyone has struggles, and frequently those who are better at hiding them are suffering a harder battle. It takes only a few seconds to be kind, and it's so worth it. With this positivity, I also want to tell readers that grief takes time. It's been almost nineteen months but it still feels like yesterday. Don't let others' expectations that you should feel fine cause you to suppress your feelings. Your journey is your own. Cry when you need to, talk when you need to, laugh when you need to, and be angry when you need to. It will pass until the next episode occurs. This is the hardest part of grief.

Nobody likes to talk about death, but I'm grateful that this book has given me the opportunity to talk about Michael. As the sibling, I frequently feel like my grief is overshadowed. The pain my brother's death has brought my parents is unimaginable, and as I have become a parent since his loss, I have a stronger sense of that loss. I am there for my parents at every opportunity, and always will be. It feels wrong for me to say that some days I wish people would see the impact the loss of my brother and best friend has had on me. Before becoming a parent, outliving him was always my bigger fear. I still can't imagine the big events of my future without him. Every day I'm asked about how my parents are since his death, but no one has asked me since the funeral. I answer their questions with a smile on my face, but it has given me the incentive to always check on the siblings after a loss, and let them know I'm thinking of them. I know it would mean the world if someone did the same for me. To whoever is reading this, your pain and your journey matter. I may not know you, but I love you, and I am always thinking and praying for you.

*

BROOKE NINNI MATTHEWS
Brooke's 31-year-old brother Timothy
died by homicide in 2012

When you lose a loved one to murder it's a loss that is so hard to fathom, and the grievers don't have anyone to turn to or talk to because many just don't understand that kind of loss. I've had many, many sleepless nights, even after creeping up on four years since the murder. I lay in bed many nights trying to close my eyes to sleep, and at that very moment I picture in my mind the how, what, why, the blood, his body, his last words. You name it, it comes to mind. It gets very frustrating to not only see that society doesn't understand your feelings, thoughts and pain, but also family and friends. I try to spread homicide awareness around to others, but even that is so difficult because it's almost nonexistence. I search high and low for homicide awareness items and such and there is nothing out there. There is awareness stuff out there, but absolutely nothing for homicide. I always said a sibling who has lost a sibling is the forgotten griever, and a griever who lost a loved one to homicide is the silent griever.

*

MICHAEL SMITH
Michael's 39-year-old brother Patrick
was killed by an impaired driver in 2007

You will never be the same. You will adapt, learn to cope, and move forward. But you will never be the same, and you shouldn't expect to. If you are lucky, as I was, you will change a little into a more mature version of yourself that looks to the future but remembers the past.

*

DAWN WOINOVICK
Dawn's 52-year-old brother
Todd died from cancer in 2013

Once it starts, remember the word "journey," because there is no destination. It's a complete ride all the way through. Yes, you will have great days and yes, you will have days you feel so alone you want to die. But hold on tight during those alone days, because they will become less and less. There are so many levels and feelings in grief, and grief healing of the heart. That piece of your heart that belonged to that loved one? They took it with them and left you with a piece of theirs. But you have to uncover a lot of pain, tears, hurt, anger, and more to find that beautiful treasure they left with you.

So may your journey be blessed, and may you unearth that piece they left for you. I am truly sorry for the pain and sadness you're going to endure, just don't ever quit because they didn't leave you empty handed.

*

The emotions of grief are universal,
but the experience of grief is not.

EMILY BARNHARDT

*

CHAPTER TWENTY

FINDING THE SUNRISE

One night after losing my daughter Aly, I had a dream. It was one of those awful, vivid nightmares where I was running in a frantic attempt to catch the sun. It was descending below the western horizon and advancing from behind was the pitch-black abyss of nightfall. It was ominous and frightening, and coming directly for me. I ran as fast as my legs could go toward the sunset, but my attempt was futile. The sun sank below the horizon, out of my reach. Oh, the looming nightfall was terrifying! But it was clear that if I wanted to see the sun ever again, I had to stop running west and instead walk east through the great nightfall of grief. For just as there would be no rainbow without the rain, the sun rises only on the other side of night.

The message was clear: it was futile to avoid my grief; I had to allow it to swallow me whole. Then, and only then, would I find my way through it and out the other side.

I remember reading in a bereavement book that if we don't allow ourselves to experience the full scope of the journey, it will come back to bite us. I couldn't fathom how it could get any worse, but I knew I didn't want to test that theory. So I gave in and allowed the grief to swallow me whole. I allowed myself to wail on my daughter's bedroom floor. I penned my deep emotions, regardless of who might read it. I created a national radio show to openly and candidly discuss our journeys with anyone who wanted to call in. And I allowed myself to sink to the bottom of the fiery pits of hell. This, in turn, lit a fire under me, so to speak, to find a way out.

Today I'm often asked how I manage my grief so well. Some assume that because I have found peace and joy, I'm simply avoiding my grief. Others believe that because I work in the bereavement field, I'm wallowing in self-pity. Well, which is it?

Neither. I miss my child with every breath I take. Just like you, I will always have my moments and triggers: the painful holidays, birthdays, death anniversaries, a song or smell that evokes an unexpected memory. But I have also found purpose, beauty and joy again. It takes hard work and determination to overcome profound grief, and it also takes the ability to let go and succumb to the journey. Do not be afraid of the tears, sorrow, and heartbreak; they are a natural reaction and imperative to our healing.

As you walk your own path, avail yourself of whatever bereavement tools ease your discomfort, for each one was created by someone who walked in your shoes and understands the heartache. While there are many wonderful resources available, what brings comfort to one person might irritate the next. Bereavement tools are not one-size-fits-all, so if one tool doesn't work, find another.

Lastly, grief is not something we get *over*, like a mountain. Rather, it is something we get *through*, like the rapids of Niagara Falls. Without the kayak and paddle. And plenty of falls. But it's also survivable. And if others have survived this wretched journey, why not me? And why not you?

1. VALIDATE YOUR EMOTIONS

The first step is to validate your emotions. When we talk about our deep heartbreak, we aren't ruminating in our sorrow or feeling sorry for ourselves. By discussing it, we are actually processing it. If we aren't allowed to process it, then it becomes silent grief. Silent grief is deadly grief.

Find a friend who will patiently listen while you discuss your loss for fifteen minutes every day. Set the timer, and ask him or her not to say anything during those fifteen minutes. Explain that it is important for you to just ramble without interruption, guidance, or judgment. You need not have the same listener each time, but practice this step <u>every</u> day.

2. COMPASSIONATE THOUGHTS

Find yourself a quiet spot. It can be your favorite chair, in your car, in your office, or even in your garden. Then clear your head and for five minutes think nothing but compassionate thoughts about yourself. Not your spouse, not your children, not your coworkers, but yourself. Having trouble? Fill in the blanks below, and then give yourself permission to really validate those positive qualities. Do this every day.

I have a _____

Example: good heart, gentle soul, witty personality

I make a _____

Example: good lasagna, potato salad, scrapbook, quilt

I'm a good_____

Example: friend, gardener, knitter, painter, poem writer

People would say I'm _____

Example: funny, kind, smart, gentle, generous, humble, creative

3. TENDER LOVING CARE

While grieving, it is important to consider yourself as being in the intensive care unit of Grief United Hospital, and treat yourself accordingly. How would nurses treat you if you were their patient in the ICU? They would be compassionate, gentle, and allow for plenty of rest. That is exactly how you should treat yourself. Also, consider soothing your physical self with tender loving care as an attentive way to honor your emotional pain. This doesn't mean you have to book an expensive massage. If wearing fuzzy blue socks offers a smidgen of comfort, then wear them unabashedly. If whipped cream on your cocoa offers a morsel of pleasure, then indulge unapologetically.

Treating our five senses to anything that offers a perception of delight might not erase the emotional heartache, but it will offer a reminder that not all pleasure is lost. List five ways you can offer yourself tender loving care, and then incorporate at least three into your day, every day. With practice, the awareness of delight eventually becomes effortless, and is an important step toward regaining joy.

TLC suggestions:

- Shower or bathe with a lovely scented soap
- Soak in a warm tub with Epsom salts or a splash of bath oil
- Wear a pair of extra soft socks
- Light a fragrant candle
- Listen to relaxing music
- Apply a rich lotion to your skin before bed
- Indulge in a few bites of your favorite treat
- Enjoy a mug of your favorite soothing herbal tea
- Add whipped cream to a steaming mug of cocoa

_____

_____

_____

_____

4. SEE THE BEAUTY

Listening to the birds outside my bedroom window every morning was something I had loved since childhood. But when Aly died, I found myself deaf and blind to the beauty around me. My world had become colorless and silent. One morning as I struggled to get out of bed, I halfheartedly noticed the birds chirping outside my bedroom window. My heart sank as I realized that they had been chirping all along, but I was now deaf to their morning melody. Panic set in as I concluded that I would never enjoy life's beauty ever again. Briefly entertaining thoughts of suicide to escape the profound pain, I quickly ruled it out. My family had been through so much already; I couldn't dump further pain on them. But in order to survive the heartbreak, I had to find a way to allow beauty back into my life.

So on that particular morning as I lay in bed, I forced myself to listen and really *hear* the birds. Every morning from that point forward, I repeated that same exercise. With persistent practice, it became easier and then eventually effortless to appreciate the birds' chirping and singsongs. Glorious beauty and sounds have once again returned to my world.

Profound grief can appear to rob our world of all beauty. Yet the truth is, despite our suffering, beauty continues to surround us. The birds continue to sing, flowers continue to bloom, the surf continues to ebb and flow. Reconnecting to our surroundings helps us to reintegrate back into our environment.

Begin by acknowledging one small pleasantry each day. Perhaps your ears register the sound of singing birds. Or you catch the faint scent of warm cookies as you walk past a bakery. Or notice the sun's illumination of a nearby red rosebush. Give yourself permission to notice one pleasantry, and allow it to *really* register.

Here are some suggestions:

- Listen to the birds sing (hearing)
- Observe pretty cloud formations (sight)
- Visit a nearby park and listen to the children (hearing)
- Notice the pretty colors of blooming flowers (sight)
- Light a fragrant candle (scent)
- See the beauty in the sunset (sight)
- Attend a local recital, concert, play, or comedy act (hearing)
- Wear luxury socks (touch)
- Wrap yourself in a soft scarf or sweater (touch)
- Indulge in whipped cream on your cocoa (taste)
- Enjoy a Hershey's chocolate kiss (taste)

5. PROTECT YOUR HEALTH

After our daughter's accident I soon found myself fighting an assortment of viruses including head colds, stomach flu, sore throats and more, compounding my already frazzled emotions. Studies show that profound grief throws our body into "flight or fight" syndrome for months and months, which is very hard on our physical bodies. Thus, it becomes critical to guard our physical health. Incorporating a few changes into our daily routine feels hard at first, but soon gets easy. Plus, a stronger physical health helps to strengthen our coping skills.

Below are a few suggestions to consider adding to your daily routine to help your physical self withstand the emotional upheaval.

- Practice good sleep hygiene
- Drink plenty of water
- Take a short walk outside every day
- Resist simple carbohydrates
- Keep a light calendar, guard your time carefully, and don't allow others to dictate and overflow your schedule

6. FIND AN OUTLET

For a long time in the grief journey, everything is painful. In the early days, just getting out of bed and taking a shower can be exhausting. Housecleaning, grocery shopping, and routine errands often take a back seat or disappear altogether. As painful as it is, it's very important to find an outlet that gets you out of bed each day. Finding something to distract you from the pain, occupy your mind, and soothe your senses can be tricky, but possible. Performing a repetitive action can calm your mood, and even result in a new craft or gifts to give.

Beginning a new outlet may feel exhausting at first, but remember that the first step is always the hardest. And you don't have to do it forever, just focus on it for the time being.

Possible activities include:

- Learn to mold chocolate or make soap
- Learn how to bead, knit, crochet, or quilt
- Volunteer at a local shelter
- Learn a new sport such as golf or kayaking
- Create a memorial garden in a forgotten part of the yard
- Join Pinterest
- Doodle or draw or color
- Mold clay
- Learn to scrapbook
- Join a book club

Grief is hell on earth. It truly is. But when walking through hell, your only option is to keep going. Eventually the hell ends, the dark night fades to dawn, and the sun begins its ascent once again.

Just keep going and you, too, will find the sunrise.

Lynda Cheldelin Fell

One smile can change a day.
One hug can change a life.
One hope can change a destiny.

LYNDA CHELDELIN FELL

*

MEET THE WRITERS

*

EMILY BAIRD-LEVINE
Emily's 43-year-old brother Don
died from a heart attack in 2004
ejbairdlevine@gmail.com

Emily Baird-Levine was born in Los Angeles, California, and raised in a small city in the San Gabriel Valley. She is the youngest of four children. She earned her B.A. degree in psychology at UC Santa Cruz and her Master's degree in social work from San Diego State University.

She met her husband, Bob, while they both worked as child protective service social workers in Santa Clara, California. She and Bob moved to Arizona right after getting married and had both their children there. Emily and family have lived in the Pacific Northwest for almost fifteen years. She has been a stay-at-home mom for over twenty years.

*

CHRISTINE BASTONE
Christine's 38-year-old sister
Liz died by suicide in 2012
C.Bastone@mail.com * www.facebook.com/CricketsPlace1

Christine Bastone is a stay-at-home mom in her forties who has only recently figured out that she wants to be a writer when she grows up! She was born in northeast Ohio and moved to Florida in May 1995. She married Angelo Bastone in July 1997. They have a son, Joshua, born in 2001 and a daughter, Katelyn, born in 2004. The four of them live together in their house at the end of a quiet street in central Florida. Christine has always loved to read, and was thrilled when her husband gave her a Kindle for Christmas in 2011. She has since read hundreds of Kindle books.

Christine is co-author of *Grief Diaries: Surviving Loss of a Sibling*, and contributed to the book, *Faces of Suicide, Volume 1,"* available on Amazon as a Kindle book. She has also been a guest on Grief Diaries Radio twice in 2014, both episodes are available on iTunes. At the time of this publication she is working on a new book called, *Advice from Tomorrow*.

*

SHANNON BOOS
Shannon's 21-year-old brother Kevin
was killed by two drunk drivers in 2015
Live Like Kevin | facebook.com/livelikekevin

Shannon Boos was born and raised in southern Florida and still lives in the Sunshine State. Being the youngest of three and the only girl, she was always described as "one of the boys." Shannon is currently studying to become a Certified Veterinary Technician to pursue her passion for animals. She currently works for an animal hospital as an ICU/ER assistant. She was very close to her brother, Kevin, who she lost to two drunk drivers, and has started Live Like Kevin, a project that encourages others to perform random acts of kindness just like Kevin did.

*

LISA FORESTBIRD
Lisa's 40-year-old brother Rob died
from a pontine hemorrhage in 2006

Lisa is the middle child sandwiched between two boys, Rob and Jim. She and Rob were Irish twins, being just fourteen months apart. She now thinks of herself as both the eldest child and the middle child. When she lost Rob, she committed to guarding Rob's heart and living for two. She lives and works in Longview, Washington, as a legal aid attorney and is the devoted mother to two furry friends. She enjoys surfing in her free time.

*
BONNIE FORSHEY
Bonnie's 54-year-old sister Eunice
died from bladder cancer in 2010
bonnieforshey@msn.com

Bonnie Forshey was born in Lewistown, Pennsylvania, and raised in New Castle, Delaware. She later moved to Swainsboro, Georgia, where she attended Emanuel County Junior College. She earned the Science Merit Award and graduated with her A.S. degree. Later she attended Gordon State College in Barnesville, Georgia, earning a B.S. in Nursing.

She spent most of her life working in medical-surgical, geriatrics, rehabilitation and long-term care facilities. Bonnie also raised two children, and worked as a nursing assistant, unit secretary, and in Medical Records while putting herself through school. Bonnie has two grandsons and currently resides in both Port Royal, Pennsylvania, and Brandon, Florida.

*

LAURA HABEDANK
Laura's brother Brian died
by suicide in 2010 at age 35
letterstobrianblog@yahoo.com * www.letterstobrianblog.com

Laura Habedank is a Minnesota native but has called Austin, Texas, home since November 2009. She works in accounting for a large printing firm where she has been employed since relocating to Texas.

In her spare time, she enjoys playing piano, singing, songwriting, and the occasional hike on the lovely greenbelt trails of Austin. She has an affinity for all things strange and, even at age forty-two, still finds whoopee cushions endlessly hilarious. She regularly consumes mass quantities of pizza and donuts while binge watching the TV series *Six Feet Under* on her couch in the company of her two geriatric cats, Bear and Bubba. In the paraphrased words of the immortal Ron Burgundy of the Channel 4 News Team, "She's kind of a big deal."

*

MARCELLA MALONE
Marcella's 20-year-old brother
Michael died by suicide in 2014

A brother is a
friend given by
nature. <3

Marcella Malone was born and raised in Marshall, Michigan. She was a middle child between two boys: Timothy, who was eight years older, and Michael who was one year younger. Growing up she loved the outdoors, sports and agriculture related activities.

Marcella is the mother of a beautiful one-year-old boy. She is currently working as a home health aide while attending Wayne State University to obtain her B.S. in psychology. Following graduation in May she plans to continue her education to receive her Master's in social work.

*

BROOKE NINNI MATTHEWS
Brooke's 31-year-old brother Timothy
died by homicide in 2012

Brooke Ninni Matthews was born in Reading, Pennsylvania, and grew up in a little town called Oley Valley with her parents, three sister and one brother. Brooke was born with a congenital heart defect and could not do the things other kids and her siblings could do, but her parents made sure she had a happy life.

She left high school at sixteen years old and started working in a sewing factory with her mother. She married her first husband at eighteen years old and divorced a year later. Brooke then met her second husband and fostered a little boy at the age of twenty-four, who is now her eighteen-year-old adopted son. Years later at the age of twenty-eight, Brooke fostered a little girl who is now her twelve-year-old adopted daughter.

Brooke and her husband will celebrate their twentieth wedding anniversary in November 2015.

*

NICKI NOBLE
Nicki's 43-year-old brother Don
died from a heart attack in 2004

Nicki Noble was born in California. Nicki attended college in Los Angeles. Nicki is married with two grown boys. Nicki enjoys traveling, reading, sewing, and spending time with family and friends.

*

BRIDGET PARK
Bridget's brother Austin died
by suicide in 2008 at age 14
www.bridgetpark.com

Bridget Park was born and raised on a cattle and sheep ranch in northern Nevada. She lost her older brother Austin in 2008 to suicide. Since then, she has learned to make the best out of this tragedy and to most importantly honor her brother by writing and publishing *Growing Young: A Memoir of Grief.*

Bridget is currently twenty years old and a student at Oklahoma State University. While on the side of being a full-time student, she engages in speaking engagements all over the country.

*

MARYELLEN ROACH
MaryEllen's 41-year-old sister Suzette
died in a car accident in 2012

MaryEllen Roach was raised on a forty-acre farm in southern Illinois where her family raised sheep and other animals. MaryEllen graduated high school in 1996 with honors. She moved to St. Louis, Missouri, at the age of nineteen where she  modeled and also worked for large companies based in St. Louis.

After the loss of her older sister and two young nieces, MaryEllen, her parents Marvin and Yvonna, her younger sister Ashley, and Ashley's husband Moi, all moved to northern California where they currently reside.

*

MICHAEL SMITH
Michael's 39-year-old brother Patrick
was killed by an impaired driver in 2007

Michael Smith was born in northern Connecticut and has lived in Atlanta, Miami Beach, and San Diego. He attended the University of Connecticut and several trade schools, and has worked in real estate and custom built furniture. In 2014 he moved back to the East Coast to be near family.

*

DAWN WOINOVICK
Dawn's 52-year-old brother
Todd died from cancer in 2013

Dawn Woinovick lives in the mountains though she considers herself a southern girl in spirit and soul. She is disabled by a pituitary tumor currently being treated with a medication known as "devil's pill," which she feels is true to its name. Reading is something she loves to do and earns free books by being a book reviewer. She says, "I look forward to meeting you all. God Bless."

It doesn't matter who you love
or how you love, but that you love.

ROD MCKUEN

*

THANK YOU

I am deeply indebted to the writers who contributed to *Grief Diaries: Surviving Loss of a Sibling*. It required a tremendous amount of courage to revisit such painful memories for the purpose of helping others, and the collective dedication to seeing this project to the end is a legacy to be proud of.

I very much appreciate author Annah Elizabeth's assistance in framing the start of each chapter. Her positivity and willingness are a breath of fresh air. I'm also grateful to our Grief Diaries village and the very lovely souls I consider dear friends, collaborative partners, mentors, and muses. I treasure each and every one of you!

There simply are no words to express how much I love my husband Jamie, our children, and our wonderfully supportive family and friends for being there through laughter and tears, and encouraging me at every turn. None of this would have been possible without their unquestioning love that continues to surround me.

Finally, I am indebted to our daughter Aly for being my biggest cheerleader in Heaven. Her bright star continues to inspire me, and I can feel her love through the thin veil that separates us as I work to offer help, healing and hope around the world. My dearest Lovey, I love you to the fartherest star and beyond. XO

Lynda Cheldelin Fell

Shared joy is doubled joy;
shared sorrow is half a sorrow.

SWEDISH PROVERB
*

BY LYNDA CHELDELIN FELL

MY STORY

When I was a kid, I wanted to be a brain surgeon. But life has a way of throwing us curve balls that force us down a different path. Sometimes those paths are most welcome, like mothering four wonderful children. My least favorite path? Losing a child. That path is a long and torturous one, and took me straight through the belly of hell.

My story began one night in 2007 when I had a vivid dream. My daughter Aly and I were passengers in a car that missed a curve in the road and sailed into a lake. The driver and I escaped the sinking car, but Aly did not. My beloved daughter was gone. The only evidence left behind was a book floating in the water where she disappeared.

Two years later, on August 5, 2009, that horrible nightmare became my reality when Aly died in a car accident. Returning home from a swim meet, the car carrying Aly was T-boned by a father coming home from work. My beautiful fifteen-year-old daughter took the brunt of the impact and died instantly. She was the only fatality.

Life couldn't get any worse, right? Wrong. Hell wasn't done with me yet. My dear sweet hubby buried his grief in the sand. He escaped into 80-hour work weeks, more wine, more food, and less talking. His blood pressure shot up, his cholesterol went off the chart, and the perfect storm arrived on June 4, 2012. My husband suddenly began drooling and couldn't speak. At age 46, my soulmate was having a major stroke.

My dear hubby lived but couldn't speak, read, or write, and his right side was paralyzed. He needed assistance just to sit up in bed. He needed full-time care. Still reeling from the loss of our daughter, I found myself again thrust into a fog of grief so thick, I couldn't see through the storm. Adrenaline and autopilot resumed their familiar place at the helm.

But I needed reassurance that the sun was on the other side of hell. As I fought my way through the storm, I discovered that helping others was a powerful way to heal my own heart. I began reaching out to individuals who were adrift and in need of a life raft. And a warm hug.

In 2013, I formed AlyBlue Media to house my mission. Comforting people who spoke my language and listening to their stories, my mission took on a life of its own and came in many forms: a radio show, film, webinars, and writing. I also hosted a national convention to bring the brokenhearted together. I had many wonderful speakers but the one who excited me most was a woman who had faced seven losses in a few short years: Martin Luther King's youngest daughter. I didn't bring Dr. Bernice King to the convention to tell us about her famous father—we already knew that story. I wanted to know how she survived.

Over the course of that weekend, I was deeply moved by complete strangers swapping stories about hardship. Touched to the core, I set out to capture them into a book series aptly named Grief Diaries. Over a hundred people in six countries shared stories in the first 8 titles published in December 2015. Now home to more than 600 writers spanning the globe, Grief Diaries has 23 titles in print. Another 10 titles are on their way and I've just launched our second series called Real Life Diaries.

Where am I today? Once a bereaved mother, always a bereaved mother. My heart is a bit like a broken teacup that has been glued back together. All the pieces are there, but they might not fit as seamlessly as they once did. Some days the glue is strong and unyielding. Other days that glue is wet, and threatens to spring a leak. Nonetheless, that teacup still holds water. Well, mostly coffee. Strong coffee.

Life can throw a really mean curveball that blindsides even the strongest. It's important to hold out hope that the sun can be found at the end of the path. But until you find it, it's comforting to know you aren't alone. And that is what my mission all about.

For the record, I have found the sun. Some days I marvel at its beauty. Other days it hides behind clouds. But I now know those days don't last forever. And my umbrella is much stronger than it used to be.

Helen Keller once said, "Walking with a friend in the dark is better than walking alone in the light." If you too are looking for the sun, visit our village for a hug and stay for the friendship. That's why we're here—to offer you a seat in our life raft until the storm passes, and the sun begins to shine once again. I'll even let you borrow my umbrella.

Lynda Cheldelin Fell

LYNDA CHELDELIN FELL

Considered a pioneer in the field of inspirational hope in the aftermath of hardship and loss, Lynda Cheldelin Fell has a passion for storytelling and producing groundbreaking projects that create a legacy of help, healing, and hope.

She is the creator of the award-winning *Grief Diaries* and *Real Life Diaries* book series, and CEO of AlyBlue Media. Her repertoire of interviews include Dr. Martin Luther King's daughter, Trayvon Martin's mother, sisters of the late Nicole Brown Simpson, Pastor Todd Burpo of Heaven Is For Real, CNN commentator Dr. Ken Druck, and other societal newsmakers on finding healing and hope in the aftermath of life's harshest challenges. She's a nominee for three 2017 WEGO Health National Patient Advocacy awards.

Lynda's own story began in 2007, when she had an alarming dream about her young teenage daughter, Aly. In the dream, Aly was a backseat passenger in a car that veered off the road and sailed into a lake. Aly sank with the car, leaving behind an open book floating face down on the water. Two years later, Lynda's dream became reality when her daughter was killed as a backseat passenger in a car accident while coming home from a swim meet. Overcome with grief, Lynda's forty-six-year-old husband suffered a major stroke that left him with severe disabilities, changing the family dynamics once again.

The following year, Lynda was invited to share her remarkable story about finding hope after loss, and she accepted. That cathartic experience inspired her to create groundbreaking projects spanning national events, radio, film and books to help others who share the same journey feel less alone. Now considered one of the foremost grief educators and healing facilitators in the United States, Lynda is dedicated to helping ordinary people share their own stories of survival and hope in the aftermath of loss.

lynda@lyndafell.com | www.lyndafell.com

ALYBLUE MEDIA TITLES

Grief Diaries: Victim Impact Statement

Grief Diaries: Hit by Impaired Driver

Grief Diaries: Surviving Loss of a Spouse

Grief Diaries: Surviving Loss of a Child

Grief Diaries: Surviving Loss of a Sibling

Grief Diaries: Surviving Loss of a Parent

Grief Diaries: Surviving Loss of an Infant

Grief Diaries: Surviving Loss of a Loved One

Grief Diaries: Surviving Loss by Suicide

Grief Diaries: Surviving Loss of Health

Grief Diaries: How to Help the Newly Bereaved

Grief Diaries: Loss by Impaired Driving

Grief Diaries: Loss by Homicide

Grief Diaries: Loss of a Pregnancy

Grief Diaries: Hello from Heaven

Grief Diaries: Grieving for the Living

Grief Diaries: Shattered

Grief Diaries: Project Cold Case

Grief Diaries: Poetry & Prose and More

Grief Diaries: Through the Eyes of Men

Grief Diaries: Will We Survive?

Real Life Diaries: Living with a Brain Injury

Real Life Diaries: Through the Eyes of DID

Real Life Diaries: Through the Eyes of an Eating Disorder

Real Life Diaries: Living with Endometriosis

Real Life Diaries: Living with Mental Illness

Grammy Visits From Heaven

Grandpa Visits From Heaven

Faith, Grief & Pass the Chocolate Pudding

Heaven Talks to Children

Color My Soul Whole

Grief Reiki

Humanity's legacy of stories and storytelling
is the most precious we have.

DORIS LESSING
*

To share your story, visit
www.griefdiaries.com
www.RealLifeDiaries.com

PUBLISHED BY ALYBLUE MEDIA
Inside every human is a story worth sharing.
www.AlyBlueMedia.com

Made in the USA
Columbia, SC
11 December 2019